THE WORD ON FAMILY

JIM BURNS
THE NATIONAL INSTITUTE OF YOUTH MINISTRY

Gospel Light is an evangelical Christian publisher dedicated to serving the local church. We believe God's vision for Gospel Light is to provide church leaders with biblical, user-friendly materials that will help them evangelize, disciple and minister to children, youth and families.

We hope this Gospel Light resource will help you discover biblical truth for your own life and help you minister to youth. God bless you in your work.

For a free catalog of resources from Gospel Light please contact your Christian supplier or call 1-800-4-GOSPEL.

PUBLISHING STAFF
William T. Greig, Publisher
Dr. Elmer L. Towns, Senior Consulting Publisher
Dr. Gary S. Greig, Senior Consulting Editor
Jill Honodel, Editor
Pam Weston, Assistant Editor
Kyle Duncan, Associate Publisher
Bayard Taylor, M.Div., Editor, Theological and Biblical Issues
Joey O'Connor, Contributing Writer
Debi Thayer, Designer

ISBN 0-8307-1727-7
© 1997 by Jim Burns
All rights reserved.
Printed in U.S.A.

All Scripture quotations, unless otherwise indicated, are taken from the *Holy Bible, New International Version®. NIV®.* Copyright © 1973, 1978, 1984 by International Bible Society. Used by permission of Zondervan Publishing House. All rights reserved.
Other versions used are:
NKJV—From the *New King James Version.* Copyright © 1979, 1980, 1982 by Thomas Nelson, Inc. Publishers. Used by permission. All rights reserved.
NASB—Scripture taken from the *New American Standard Bible,* © 1960, 1962, 1963, 1968, 1971, 1972, 1973, 1975, 1977 by The Lockman Foundation. Used by permission.

HOW TO MAKE CLEAN COPIES FROM THIS BOOK

YOU MAY MAKE COPIES OF PORTIONS OF THIS BOOK WITH A CLEAN CONSCIENCE IF:

- you (or someone in your organization) are the original purchaser;
- you are using the copies you make for a noncommercial purpose (such as teaching or promoting your ministry) within your church or organization;
- you follow the instructions provided in this book.

HOWEVER, IT IS **ILLEGAL** FOR YOU TO MAKE COPIES IF:

- you are using the material to promote, advertise or sell a product or service other than for ministry fund-raising;
- you are using the material in or on a product for sale;
- you or your organization are **not** the original purchaser of this book.

By following these guidelines you help us keep our products affordable.
Thank you,
Gospel Light

Permission to make photocopies or to reproduce by any other mechanical or electronic means in whole or in part of any designated* page, illustration or activity in this book is granted only to the original purchaser and is intended for noncommercial use within a church or other Christian organization. None of the material in this book may be reproduced for any commercial promotion, advertising or sale of a product or service. Sharing of the material in this book with other churches or organizations not owned or controlled by the original purchaser is also prohibited. All rights reserved.

*Pages with the following notation can be legally reproduced:
© 1997 by Gospel Light. Permission to photocopy granted. *The Word on Family*

Praise for YouthBuilders

Jim Burns knows young people. He also knows how to communicate to them. This study should be in the hands of every youth leader interested in discipling young people.
David Adams, Vice President, Lexington Baptist College

I deeply respect and appreciate the groundwork Jim Burns has prepared for true teenage discernment. *YouthBuilders* is timeless in the sense that the framework has made it possible to plug into any society, at any point in time, and to proceed to discuss, experience and arrive at sincere moral and Christian conclusions that will lead to growth and life changes. Reaching young people may be more difficult today than ever before, but God's grace is alive and well in Jim Burns and this wonderful curriculum.
Fr. Angelo J. Artemas, Youth Ministry Director, Greek Orthodox Archdiocese of North and South America

I heartily recommend Jim Burns's *YouthBuilders Group Bible Studies* because they are leader-friendly tools that are ready to use in youth groups and Sunday School classes. Jim addresses the tough questions that students are genuinely facing every day and, through his engaging style, challenges young people to make their own decisions to move from their current opinions to God's convictions taught in the Bible. Every youth group will benefit from this excellent curriculum.
Paul Borthwick, Minister of Missions, Grace Chapel

Jim Burns recognizes the fact that small groups are where life change happens. In this study he has captured the essence of that value. Further, Jim has given much thought to shaping this very effective material into a usable tool that serves the parent, leader and student.
Bo Boshers, Executive Director, Student Impact, Willow Creek Community Church

It is about time that someone who knows kids, understands kids and works with kids writes youth curriculum that youth workers, both volunteer and professional, can use. Jim Burns's *YouthBuilders Group Bible Studies* is the curriculum that youth ministry has been waiting a long time for.
Ridge Burns, President,
The Center for Student Missions

Jim Burns has done it again. He speaks to kids right where they are and helps them to understand what Christianity is about in their own terms.
Tony Campolo, Professor, Eastern College

There are very few people in the world who know how to communicate life-changing truth effectively to teens. Jim Burns is one of the best. *YouthBuilders Group Bible Studies* puts handles on those skills and makes them available to everyone. These studies are biblically sound, hands-on practical and just plain fun. This one gets a five-star endorsement—which isn't bad since there are only four stars to start with.
Ken Davis, President, Dynamic Communications

I don't know anyone who knows and understands the needs of the youth worker like Jim Burns. His new curriculum not only reveals his knowledge of youth ministry but also his depth and sensitivity to the Scriptures. *YouthBuilders Group Bible Studies* is solid, easy to use and gets students out of their seats and into the Word. I've been waiting for something like this for a long time!
Doug Fields, Pastor of High School, Saddleback Valley Community Church

Jim Burns has a way of being creative without being "hokey." *YouthBuilders Group Bible Studies* takes the age-old model of curriculum and gives it a new look with tools such as the Bible *Tuck-In*™ and Parent Page. Give this new resource a try and you'll see that Jim shoots straightforward on tough issues. The *YouthBuilders* series is great for leading small-group discussions as well as teaching a large class of junior high or high school students. The Parent Page will help you get support from your parents in that they will understand the topics you are dealing with in your group. Put Jim's years of experience to work for you by equipping yourself with this quality material.
Curt Gibson, Pastor to Junior High, First Church of the Nazarene of Pasadena

Once again, Jim Burns has managed to handle very timely issues with just the right touch. His *YouthBuilders Group Bible Studies* succeeds in teaching solid biblical values without being stuffy or preachy. The format is user-friendly, designed to stimulate high involvement and deep discussion. Especially impressive is the Parent Page, a long overdue tool to help parents become part of the Christian education loop. I look forward to using it with my kids!
David M. Hughes, Pastor, First Baptist Church, Winston-Salem

What do you get when you combine a deep love for teens, over 20 years' experience in youth ministry and an excellent writer? You get Jim Burns's *YouthBuilders* series! This stuff has absolutely hit the nail on the head. Quality Sunday School and small-group material is tough to come by these days, but Jim has put every ounce of creativity he has into these books.
Greg Johnson, author of
Getting Ready for the Guy/Girl Thing and
Keeping Your Cool While Sharing Your Faith

Jim Burns has a gift, the gift of combining the relational and theological dynamics of our faith in a graceful, relevant and easy-to-chew-and-swallow way. *YouthBuilders Group Bible Studies* is a hit, not only for teens but for teachers.
Gregg Johnson, National Youth Director, International Church of the Foursquare Gospel

The practicing youth worker always needs more ammunition. Here is a whole book full of practical, usable resources for those facing kids face-to-face. *YouthBuilders Group Bible Studies* will get that blank stare off the faces of kids in your youth meeting!
Jay Kesler, President, Taylor University

I couldn't be more excited about the *YouthBuilders Group Bible Studies*. It couldn't have arrived at a more needed time. Spiritually we approach the future engaged in war with young people taking direct hits from the devil. This series will practically help teens who feel partially equipped to "put on the whole armor of God."
Mike MacIntosh, Pastor,
Horizon Christian Fellowship

In *YouthBuilders Group Bible Studies*, Jim Burns pulls together the key ingredients for an effective curriculum series. Jim captures the combination of teen involvement and a solid biblical perspective, with topics that are relevant and straightforward. This series will be a valuable tool in the local church.
Dennis "Tiger" McLuen, Executive Director, Youth Leadership

My ministry takes me to the lost kids in our nation's cities where youth games and activities are often irrelevant and plain Bible knowledge for the sake of learning is unattractive. Young people need the information necessary to make wise decisions related to everyday problems. *YouthBuilders* will help many young people integrate their faith into everyday life, which after all is our goal as youth workers.
Miles McPherson, President, Project Intercept

Jim Burns's passion for teens, youth workers and parents of teens is evident in the *YouthBuilders Group Bible Studies*. He has a gift of presenting biblical truths on a level teens will fully understand, and youth workers and parents can easily communicate.
Al Menconi, President, Al Menconi Ministries

Youth ministry curriculum is often directed to only one spoke of the wheel of youth ministry—the adolescent. Not so with this material! Jim has enlarged the education circle, including information for the adolescent, the parent and the youth worker. *YouthBuilders Group Bible Studies* is youth and family ministry-oriented material at its best.
Helen Musick, Instructor of Youth Ministry, Asbury Seminary

Finally, a Bible study that has it all! It's action-packed, practical and biblical; but that's only the beginning. *YouthBuilders* involves students in the Scriptures. It's relational, interactive and leads kids toward lifestyle changes. The unique aspect is a page for parents, something that's usually missing from adolescent curriculum. Jim Burns has outdone himself. This isn't a home run—it's a grand slam!
Dr. David Olshine, Director of Youth Ministries, Columbia International University

Here is a thoughtful and relevant curriculum designed to meet the needs of youth workers, parents and students. It's creative, interactive and biblical—and with Jim Burns's name on it, you know you're getting a quality resource.
Laurie Polich, Youth Director, First Presbyterian Church of Berkeley

In 10 years of youth ministry I've never used a curriculum because I've never found anything that actively involves students in the learning process, speaks to young people where they are and challenges them with biblical truth—I'll use this! *YouthBuilders Group Bible Studies* is a complete curriculum that is helpful to parents, youth leaders and, most importantly, today's youth.
Glenn Schroeder, Youth and Young Adult Ministries, Vineyard Christian Fellowship, Anaheim

This new material by Jim Burns represents a vitality in curriculum and, I believe, a more mature and faithful direction. *YouthBuilders Group Bible Studies* challenges youth by teaching them how to make decisions rather than telling them what decisions to make. Each session offers teaching concepts, presents options and asks for a decision. I believe it's healthy, the way Christ taught and represents the abilities, personhood and faithfulness of youth. I give it an *A+*!
J. David Stone, President, Stone & Associates

Jim Burns has done it again! This is a practical, timely and reality-based resource for equipping teens to live life in the fast-paced, pressure-packed adolescent world of the '90s. A very refreshing creative oasis in the curriculum desert!
Rich Van Pelt, President, Alongside Ministries

YouthBuilders Group Bible Studies is a tremendous new set of resources for reaching students. Jim has his finger on the pulse of youth today. He understands their mind-sets, and has prepared these studies in a way that will capture their attention and lead to greater maturity in Christ. I heartily recommend these studies.
Rick Warren, Senior Pastor,
Saddleback Valley Community Church

CONTENTS

Thanks and Thanks Again! 10
Dedication 11
How to Use this Study 12
A Special Note from Jim Burns 14

Unit I Communication 15

    Session 1 Communicating 17
        Good communication is the key to healthy relationships in any family.

    Session 2 Family Roles and Goals 29
        When biblical principles are implemented in the home, stronger, healthier relationships are developed.

    Session 3 Expressing Appreciation 41
        Family members need to express words of encouragement to one another often.

    Session 4 The Power of Being There 51
        Family members regard your very presence as a sign of caring and connectedness.

Unit II Respect 61

    Session 5 Honor and Obey 63
        God's command is to honor and obey our parents. Obeying His command will be rewarded.

    Session 6 Walking in Your Parents' Shoes 75
        In order to have healthy relationships with our parents, we sometimes need to understand why they act the way they do.

    Session 7 A Tribute to Mom 87
        Your mom is a gift from God. She is to be affirmed and honored.

    Session 8 A Father's Love 99
        A father's love comes in all shapes and sizes, but it's not always perfect. However, our heavenly Father is always approachable, and His love is both sacrificial *and* perfect.

Unit III Stress 113

    Session 9 Resolving Conflict 115
        When biblical principles are properly applied to resolving conflict, family relationships become healthier and communication is clearer.

    Session 10 Frazzled Families 125
        Thriving families seek God first and set their priorities by His standards. Frazzled families are unfocused and too busy to develop strong relationships with one another and with God.

    Session 11 Divorce 139
        Divorce results in loss. Understanding the issues involved in divorce helps its victims find healing.

    Session 12 Family Crises 151
        Every family experiences crises at one time or another. There are biblical answers to help anyone working through these difficult times.

THANKS AND THANKS AGAIN!

This project is definitely a team effort. First of all, thank you to Cathy, Christy, Rebecca and Heidi Burns, the women of my life.

Thank you to Jill Corey, my incredible assistant and longtime friend.

Thank you to the NIYM staff in San Clemente, Russ Cline, Larry Acosta, Dean Bruns and Wendi Matlock, Diana Spitz and Lori Nellis.

Thank you to our 250-plus associate trainers who have been my coworkers, friends and sacrificial guinea pigs.

Thank you to Kyle Duncan and Bill Greig III for convincing me that Gospel Light is a great publisher that deeply believes in the mission to reach kids. I believe!

Thank you to the Youth Specialties world: Tic, Mike and Wayne, you, so many years ago, brought on a wet-behind-the-ears youth worker and taught me most everything I know about youth work today.

Thank you to the hundreds of donors, supporters and friends of the National Institute of Youth Ministry. You are helping create an international grassroots movement that is helping young people make positive decisions that will affect them for the rest of their lives.

A very special thanks and acknowledgment to the James L. Stamps Foundation. Your friendship and support for this project and others has made an eternal difference.

"Where there is no counsel, the people fall; but in the multitude of counselors there is safety" (Proverbs 11:14, *NKJV*).

Jim Burns
San Clemente, California

DEDICATION

For my incredible family of women!

Cathy, your unwavering commitment to our family is an inspiration and the dividends are paying off.

Christy, you are my world's most wonderful teenager. This book has you written all over it.

Rebecca, you are beautiful on the outside and inside. You continue to teach our family so much about compassion for others, faith, fun and joy.

Heidi, attitude is everything and you have the best in the universe. I'm proud to be your Dad.

I would once again like to thank my executive assistant, Jill Corey, who not only does a phenomenal job but is a treasured part of our family. Thank you Jill, for your invaluable part in this three-year project.

YOUTHBUILDERS GROUP BIBLE STUDIES

It's Relational—Students learn best when they talk, not when you talk. There is always a get-acquainted section in the Warm Up. All the experiences are based on building community in your group.

It's Biblical—With no apologies, this series is unashamedly Christian. Every session has a practical, relevant Bible study.

It's Experiential—Studies show that young people retain up to 85 percent of the material when they are *involved* in action-oriented, experiential learning. The sessions use role-plays, discussion starters, case studies, graphs and other experiential, educational methods. *We believe it's a sin to bore a young person with the gospel.*

It's Interactive—This study is geared to get students feeling comfortable with sharing ideas and interacting with peers and leaders.

It's Easy to Follow—The sessions have been prepared by Jim Burns to allow the leader to pick up the material and use it. There is little preparation time on your part. Jim did the work for you.

It's Adaptable—You can pick and choose from several topics or go straight through the material as a whole study.

It's Age Appropriate—In the "Team Effort" section, one group experience relates best to junior high students while the other works better with high school students. Look at both to determine which option is best for your group.

It's Parent Oriented—The Parent Page helps you to do youth ministry at its finest. Christian education should take place in the home as well as in the church. The Parent Page is your chance to come alongside the parents and help them have a good discussion with their kids.

It's Proven—This material was not written by someone in an ivory tower. It was written for young people and has already been used with them. They love it.

HOW TO USE THIS STUDY

The 12 sessions are divided into three stand-alone units. Each unit has four sessions. You may choose to teach all 12 sessions consecutively. Or you may use only one unit. Or you may present individual sessions. You know your best so you choose.

Each of the 12 sessions is divided into five sections.

Warm Up—Young people will stay in your youth group if they feel comfortable and make friends in the group. This section is designed for you and the students to get to know each other better. These activities are filled with history-giving and affirming questions and experiences.

Team Effort—Following the model of Jesus, the Master Teacher, these activities engage young people in the session. Stories, group situations, surveys and more bring the session to the students. There is an option for junior high/middle school students and one for high school students.

In the Word—Most young people are biblically illiterate. These Bible studies present the Word of God and encourage students to see the relevance of the Scriptures to their lives.

Things to Think About—Young people need the opportunity to really think through the issues at hand. These discussion starters get students talking about the subject and interacting on important issues.

Parent Page—A youth worker can only do so much. Reproduce this page and get it into the hands of parents. This tool allows quality parent/teen communication that really brings the session home.

THE BIBLE *TUCK-IN*™

It's a tear-out sheet you fold and place in your Bible, containing the essentials you'll need for teaching your group.

Here's How to Use It:

To prepare for the session, first study the session. Tear out the Bible *Tuck-In*™ and personalize it by making notes. Fold the Bible *Tuck-In*™ in half on the dotted line. Slip it into your Bible for easy reference throughout the session. The Key Verse, Biblical Basis and Big Idea at the beginning of the Bible *Tuck-In*™ will help you keep the session on track. With the Bible *Tuck-In*™ your students will see that your teaching comes from the Bible and won't be distracted by a leader's guide.

A Special Note from Jim Burns

Cathy and I both grew up in traditional two-parent families. Although we wouldn't consider our homes perfect, we now realize that living in a two-parent family without the stresses of divorce, death, abuse or blending families is a blessing not necessarily experienced by many today. Even the fact that both of our moms stayed home is not the norm. Actually, what I mean to say is that the majority of young people that you and I will work with now and in the future will not be from what was at one time the normal family with a dad, a mom, kids and a dog, and maybe even a white picket fence.

Today when we think of family, we must realize that the kids we are serving come from almost every type of family situation possible. Some may be scarred by varying degrees of dysfunction in their families. Many don't have both parents in the home and others have had several dads or moms. Trying to blend two or more families together to become one causes some rough edges that hurt a lot when they scrape against one another in the process. Today many students are torn between two or three families every day of their lives. What's even worse is that the tension is often magnified during holidays or special events in their lives when others are enjoying a spirit of celebration.

Needless to say as you approach this most important subject, you will want to be especially sensitive and caring when it comes to these family issues. This book will unashamedly celebrate the biblical standards for families and hopefully many of your students will choose the godly pattern for their future families. The important teaching point is to be as inclusive as Christ would be toward kids who believe they have a less-than-perfect family. I know you will punctuate each session with God's grace and love. The beauty of youth ministry is that although we can never replace the biological families of our students, we can offer them the fellowship of the family of God and a life-changing relationship with their perfect heavenly Father.

Unit 1

COMMUNICATION

Leader's Pep Talk

My daughter Rebecca invited me to be her show-and-tell for her third-grade class.

I asked her, "Are the other daddys also coming to show and tell?"

"No, just you, Dad," was her reply.

Well this was one speaking gig that made me quite nervous. "What do you want me to say? Would you like me to share what I do?"

"No Dad, just come and I'll share you."

When the day arrived, I had to speak to a high school assembly on sexuality that morning, and I was hardly nervous. But as I started driving to my daughter's class, I could feel the nerves working overtime. *What would I say? Would I make Rebecca proud?* I walked into the class. The children stopped what they were doing, turned and looked at me. Rebecca got up from her seat, led me to the front of the class and introduced me. "This is my dad. His name is Jim. He's a great guy and he is bald!" (As if they couldn't tell!)

I talked for a few minutes and then the children asked questions. Every kid put his or her hand up to ask a question. Matthew asked how old I was and Mallory wanted to know if we had a dog. Most of the questions were about my family and none of them were about my work.

When it was all finished, little Rebecca put her arms around me and said, "Thanks for coming to my class, Daddy. I'm so proud of you."

Wow! What a day. As I got back into my car to go to my office, I realized that my daughter and her friends didn't care much about my academic degrees or how much money I make. Their questions were personal and relational. It helped me realize that my daughter isn't impressed that I write or speak to students. For Rebecca the power of me being there for her is what counts. She just likes to spend time with me.

This first section is about communicating, understanding and appreciation. I hope your students will finish this section with a greater appreciation for their parents and with the biblical communication skills needed for healthy relationships. God designed the family to love and be loved. In His design, the family is the central factor in bringing faith to children and in helping them know their roots.

As a youth worker you have the privilege of helping your students have closer relationships with and better understandings of their families. Many issues of the day will fade, but strong family units are essential to the quality of our lives. Thank you for helping kids develop better families. You have an important task.

SESSION ONE

COMMUNICATING

KEY VERSE

"Whatever you do, whether in word or deed, do it all in the name of the Lord Jesus, giving thanks to God the Father through him." Colossians 3:17

BIBLICAL BASIS

Proverbs 12:18;
Colossians 3:12-17

THE BIG IDEA

Good communication is the key to healthy relationships in any family.

AIMS OF THIS SESSION

During this session you will guide students to:
- Examine practical ways for better communication in their families;
- Discover new communication skills;
- Implement a plan to communicate more clearly with their families.

WARM UP

SOLVE THE PROBLEM—
Students discuss ways to improve communication in families.

TEAM EFFORT— JUNIOR HIGH/ MIDDLE SCHOOL

COMMUNICATION STYLES—
Students role-play situations illustrating different communication styles.

TEAM EFFORT— HIGH SCHOOL

COMMUNICATION PRINCIPLES—
Discussion of the barriers to communication plus the basic guidelines and goals of good communication principles.

IN THE WORD

COMMUNICATION WITH YOUR FAMILY—
A Bible study on how to improve family communication.

THINGS TO THINK ABOUT (OPTIONAL)

Questions to get students thinking and talking about how to improve communication in their families.

PARENT PAGE

A tool to get the session into the home and allow parents and young people to practice using phrases that enhance communication.

SESSION ONE

COMMUNICATING

LEADER'S DEVOTIONAL

"Reckless words pierce like a sword, but the tongue of the wise brings healing" (Proverbs 12:18).

"Before I tell you anything, you have to promise *not* to tell my parents."

"If my son or daughter knew I was speaking with you, they'd have an absolute fit. Promise me you won't tell them that we spoke."

Feeling stuck in the middle? Second Corinthians was uncannily right—you are an ambassador for Christ, a diplomat in the finest sense of the word, an international statesman representing both sides of two conflict-ridden interest groups marred by confusing language and authority problems: parents and teenagers. Talk about conflict of interests!

As a youth worker you have the precarious position of representing the interests of both the young people and parents you serve. You ride the proverbial fence of winning the hearts of teenagers for Christ and the respect/approval/help/support/fill-in-the-blank _____ of the parents you also serve. In short, you are not just a youth minister. Nor are you just an every-so-often-whenever-a-need-arises minister to parents. Full-time, part-time, volunteer—you are a minister to families.

Good communication is a key sign of a healthy family, and one of your most important roles is to help facilitate positive communication between parents and teenagers. You are often called to be the oil to reduce the friction and heat resulting from family conflicts, misunderstandings and crises. If you feel stuck in the middle between wondering who to stick up for between the warring sides of a parent and teenager conflict, take a moment to stand back from the situation and remember that your role is to be pro-family. You are looking out for the best interests of parents *and* teenagers. Except in cases of physical, emotional or sexual abuse, you are a type of spiritual Switzerland. Neutral. Objective. Unbiased. You are there to help promote the growth of every family member.

There is no such thing as a professional parent, a totally-together teenager or an ideal family like the one Wally and the Beav had. In one way, every family is in the tricky process of trying to figure out what it means to be a family. That's why your role in helping facilitate healthy communication is so critical to the families in your ministry. This session is filled with fantastic ideas to help parents and teenagers better communicate with one another. By promoting these ideas and concepts with the families in your ministry, not only will you assist parents and teenagers in learning how to handle their inevitable conflicts, but you will help them lay a strong foundation for healthy communication in the future. (Written by Joey O'Connor)

"The difference between the right word and the almost right word is the difference between lightning and the lightning bug."
—Mark Twain

SESSION ONE BIBLE TUCK-IN™

COMMUNICATING

Key Verse

"Whatever you do, whether in word or deed, do it all in the name of the Lord Jesus, giving thanks to God the Father through him." Colossians 3:17

Biblical Basis

Proverbs 12:18; Colossians 3:12-17

The Big Idea

Good communication is the key to healthy relationships in any family.

Warm Up (5-10 Minutes)

Solve the Problem
- Divide students into at least three groups.
- Give each group a copy of "Solve the Problem" on page 21, or display a copy using an overhead projector. Assign one situation to each group.
- Have each group read and discuss the assigned communication problem and the advice they would give.
- If time allows, have each group share the advice they would give in each situation. Read the situation that has been assigned to your group, then discuss the question.

A. Linda and Jerry's dad comes home from work every evening and immediately slumps into his favorite chair. He turns on the TV, absentmindedly pets the dog and reads the newspaper. Linda and Jerry believe he pays more attention to their dog than to them.
What advice would you give Linda and Jerry?

B. Sue talks all the time and everyone knows where she stands on every subject. Her younger brother Steve, however, is much more quiet. Basically no one knows what he is thinking.
What advice would you give to their family to create better communication between all members?

---Fold---

For Better Personal Communication:
1. Be open to communicating. Listen attentively.
2. Look the person in the eye.
3. Touch the person when appropriate.
4. Imagine what the other person is going through. Be willing to feel their emotions.
5. Linger, take the time to understand one another.
6. Be honest.
7. Speak only for yourself.
8. Be yourself.
9. Expect nothing in return.
10. Be willing to say "I don't know."
11. Be willing to say "I'm sorry."
12. Ask the second question.
13. Don't expect to solve major relationship problems in one conversation.
14. Have a caring attitude.
15. Believe in the worth of the other person.
16. Be humble.
17. Be an active listener.
18. Make communication a priority.
19. Pick a time and place that will make communication easier.
20. Focus on one issue at a time rather than many issues.
21. Don't use phrases such as "You never" or "You always" because this is *always never* true!

In what ways are you a good communicator?

How can you improve your communication?

Things to Think About (optional)

- Use the questions on page 27 after or as a part of "In the Word."
1. What are ways your family has solved a communication problem?

2. Why is it often a difficult thing to communicate with someone you love?

3. How can put-downs and irritability cause the communication gates to close?

When have you felt put down? How does it affect your relationship with the one putting you down?

Do you tend to put down others? What is your motive?

Parent Page

- Distribute page to parents.

19

C. Barbara is very defensive. Whenever her mother questions any of her behavior, she yells at her mom and goes way overboard being defensive.
What advice would you give their family?

Team Effort—Junior High/Middle School (15-20 Minutes)

Communication Styles
- Divide students into groups of two or three.
- Give each group a copy of "Communication Styles" on page 22 or display a copy using an overhead projector.
- Assign each group a communication style. Give a brief description for each style.
- Give the groups five minutes to develop dramatic role plays based on the situation of deciding what movie to see, illustrating their assigned communication styles.
- Have the groups present their role plays for one another.
- After each group has presented its role play, discuss the questions.

Questions:
How could the negative communication in this role play be turned into a positive communication experience?

Team Effort—High School (15-20 Minutes)

Communication Principles
- Divide students into groups of three or four.
- Give each student a copy of "Communication Principles" on page 23 and a pen or pencil.
- Have students check off statements that apply to their own families as you read through the principles.
- Have one person in each group suggest a communication problem he or she has encountered, then the small groups will discuss how to solve the problem using these principles.

In The Word (25-30 Minutes)

Communicating with Your Family
- Divide students into groups of three or four.
- Give each student a copy of "Communicating with Your Family" on pages 24-26 and a pen or pencil, or display the page using an overhead projector.
- Have students complete the study with their small groups.
Read the following Scripture in unison:

"Therefore, as God's chosen people, holy and dearly loved, clothe yourselves with compassion, kindness, humility, gentleness and patience. Bear with each other and forgive whatever grievances you may have against one another. Forgive as the Lord forgave you. And over all these virtues put on love, which binds them all together in perfect unity.

"Let the peace of Christ rule in your hearts, since as members of one body you were called to peace. And be thankful. Let the word of Christ dwell in you richly as you teach and admonish one another with all wisdom, and as you sing psalms, hymns and spiritual songs with gratitude in your hearts to God. And whatever you do, whether in word or deed, do it all in the name of the Lord Jesus, giving thanks to God the Father through him" (Colossians 3:12-17).

Circle the words in this powerful Scripture that will help to improve communication in your family.
What principles, words or phrases would, if applied to your family life, improve communication?

Which verse(s) do you need to apply when you communicate?

With this Scripture in mind, let's think through the following important communication principles:

Communication Is A Key!
In order to improve relationships, everyone must constantly work on improving the communication process.
List several things you can do to communicate better with other family members.

Review your list and circle two experiences you will try to work on this week.

Spend Time with Your Parents
You are very important to your parents. As you get older, they still eagerly desire to spend time with you.
If it has been a while since you have gone out to dinner with your parents, or shopping, or to a ball game, or some other activity, then it is time you asked them for a "date."

List four different things you could do to spend time with your parents. (Examples: have lunch with Mom, go to a ball game with Dad, stay home every Monday for family games, etc.)

Mom	Dad
1.	1.
2.	2.
3.	3.
4.	4.

List four different things you could do to spend time with other family members. (Examples: play a game with a younger brother or sister, help an older brother or sister do the dishes, etc.)

1.
2.
3.
4.

So What?
- Note to leader: Before students begin this section, briefly share with the whole group an example from your own life in which you could have communicated more effectively.

Have each person in your small group suggest a specific family communication problem. Read the following personal communication guidelines and write each person's initials beside the ones that will help resolve each communication problem.

SESSION ONE

 COMMUNICATING

SOLVE THE PROBLEM

Read the situation that has been assigned to your group and then discuss the question.

A. Linda and Jerry's dad comes home from work every evening and immediately slumps into his favorite chair. He turns on the TV, absentmindedly pets the dog and reads the newspaper. Linda and Jerry believe he pays more attention to their dog than to them.

What advice would you give Linda and Jerry?

....
....
....

B. Sue talks all the time and everyone knows where she stands on every subject. Her younger brother Steve, however, is much more quiet. Basically no one knows what he is thinking.

What advice would you give to their family to create better communication between all members?

....
....
....

C. Barbara is very defensive. Whenever her mother questions any of her behavior she yells at her mom and goes way overboard being defensive.

What advice would you give their family?

....
....
....

© 1997 by Gospel Light. Permission to photocopy granted. *The Word on Family*

SESSION ONE

COMMUNICATING

Team Effort

COMMUNICATION STYLES

The following is a list of negative communication styles:

The Preaching Parent delivers a sermon rather than listening to the student's needs.

The Silent Loner does not share feelings, thoughts and needs, retreating from others to avoid conflict.

The Stubborn Hardhead will not listen to another's point of view, will not compromise and insists he or she is always right.

The Angry Rebel automatically strikes out in anger at any one else's suggestion and wants to do the opposite of everyone else.

The Macho Maniac tries to take charge of everything and throw his or her weight around.

The Laughing Clown makes a joke of everything, including the ideas, feelings and desires of others.

The Super-Submissive Servant does whatever everyone else suggests and never expresses his or her own opinions.

The Martyr gives in to others, but makes sure others know of his or her "sacrifice."

The Demander always has to have his or her own way.

The Whiner agrees to do what others want but complains about the decision the whole time.

Questions:

What was the negative communication in this role play?

....
....
....

How could this situation be turned into a positive communication experience?

....
....
....

© 1997 by Gospel Light. Permission to photocopy granted. *The Word on Family*

SESSION ONE

COMMUNICATING

Team Effort

COMMUNICATION PRINCIPLES

Communication is a key to any relationship and is a must for quality family relationships. Read these key communications principles and make a check beside any statements that apply to your family.

Basics of Good Communication
- ❏ Some try to communicate rules rather than have a relationship.
- ❏ Who you are communicates more than what you do.
- ❏ What you do communicates more than what you say.
- ❏ You must be working to improve yourself before you can help someone else.
- ❏ Quality people produce quality communication.
- ❏ Others _____

Barriers to Good Communication
- ❏ Lack of time
- ❏ Failure to make communication a priority
- ❏ Media: TV, radio, music, videos
- ❏ Twentieth-century rush
- ❏ Guilt
- ❏ Anger
- ❏ Stubborn natures
- ❏ Memories of past rejection
- ❏ Feelings of inferiority, low self-esteem and worthlessness
- ❏ Misplaced anger—taking out anger at others on those closest to you
- ❏ Drugs and alcohol
- ❏ Rules vs. relationship

What are other possible barriers to communication?

....
....
....

Goals of Quality Communication
- ❏ Mutual understanding
- ❏ Expression of care, concern and love
- ❏ Sharing yourself
- ❏ Expression of needs
- ❏ Motivation to change
- ❏ Demonstrate acceptance

Now have someone in your small group suggest a problem. With these principles in mind, discuss how to solve the problem through better communication.

© 1997 by Gospel Light. Permission to photocopy granted. *The Word on Family*

SESSION ONE

COMMUNICATING

In the Word

COMMUNICATING WITH YOUR FAMILY

Read the following Scripture in unison:

> "Therefore, as God's chosen people, holy and dearly loved, clothe yourselves with compassion, kindness, humility, gentleness and patience. Bear with each other and forgive whatever grievances you may have against one another. Forgive as the Lord forgave you. And over all these virtues put on love, which binds them all together in perfect unity.
>
> "Let the peace of Christ rule in your hearts, since as members of one body you were called to peace. And be thankful. Let the word of Christ dwell in you richly as you teach and admonish one another with all wisdom, and as you sing psalms, hymns and spiritual songs with gratitude in your hearts to God. And whatever you do, whether in word or deed, do it all in the name of the Lord Jesus, giving thanks to God the Father through him" (Colossians 3:12-17).

Circle the words in this powerful Scripture that will help you to improve communication in your family.

What principles, words or phrases would, if applied to your family life, improve communication?

....
....
....

Which verse(s) do you need to apply when you communicate?

....
....

With this Scripture in mind, let's think through the following important communication principles:

Communication Is a Key!

In order to improve relationships, everyone must constantly work on improving the communication process.

List several things you can do to communicate better with your parents.

....
....
....
....

Review your list above and circle two experiences you will try to work on this week.

SESSION ONE

COMMUNICATING

List several things you can do to communicate better with other family members.

....
....
....
....
....

Review your list above and circle two experiences you will try to work on this week.

Spend Time with Your Parents

You are very important to your parents. As you get older they still eagerly desire to spend time with you.

If it has been a while since you have gone out to dinner with your parents, or shopping, or to a ball game, or some other activity, then it is time you asked them for a "date."

List four different things you could do to spend time with your parents. (Examples: have lunch with Mom, go to a ball game with Dad, stay home every Monday for family games, etc.)

Mom	Dad
1.	1.
2.	2.
3.	3.
4.	4.

List four different things you could do to spend time with other family members. (Examples: play a game with a younger brother or sister, help an older brother or sister do the dishes, etc.)

_____	_____
1.	1.
2.	2.
3.	3.
4.	4.

© 1997 by Gospel Light. Permission to photocopy granted. *The Word on Family*

SESSION ONE

COMMUNICATING

So What?

Have each person in your small group suggest a specific family communication problem. Read the following personal communication guidelines and write each person's initials beside the ones that will help resolve each communication problem.

For Better Personal Communication

_____ 1. Be open to communicating. Listen attentively.
_____ 2. Look the person in the eye.
_____ 3. Touch the person when appropriate.
_____ 4. Imagine what the other person is going through. Be willing to feel their emotions.
_____ 5. Linger, take the time to understand one another.
_____ 6. Be honest.
_____ 7. Speak only for yourself.
_____ 8. Be yourself.
_____ 9. Expect nothing in return.
_____ 10. Be willing to say "I don't know."
_____ 11. Be willing to say "I'm sorry."
_____ 12. Ask the second question.
_____ 13. Don't expect to solve major relationship problems in one conversation.
_____ 14. Have a caring attitude.
_____ 15. Believe in the worth of the other person.
_____ 16. Be humble.
_____ 17. Be an active listener.
_____ 18. Make communication a priority.
_____ 19. Pick a time and place that will make communication easier.
_____ 20. Focus on one issue at a time rather than many issues.
_____ 21. Don't use phrases such as "You never" or "You always" because this is *always never* true!

In what ways are you a good communicator?

....
....
....

How can you improve your communication?

....
....
....

© 1997 by Gospel Light. Permission to photocopy granted. *The Word on Family*

SESSION ONE

COMMUNICATING

Things to Think About

1. What are ways your family has solved a communication problem?

2. Why is it often a difficult thing to communicate with someone you love?

3. How can put-downs and irritability cause the communication gates to close?

    When have you felt put down? How does it affect your relationship with the one putting you down?

    Do you tend to put down others? What is your motive?

SESSION ONE

COMMUNICATING

Parent Page

WORDS AND PHRASES THAT AID COMMUNICATION

Here are 17 great phrases to enhance communication. Have each family member choose five phrases they would like to say. Have each person tell the other family members one phrase he or she has chosen and why. After everyone has shared one phrase, have them share the second phrases they have chosen.

I love you.	I care about you.
I need you.	You are special.
What do you think?	How do you feel about it?
What would you do?	I've got a problem.
I need your help.	I blew it.
I made a mistake.	I'm sorry.
I want you to forgive me.	I want to make things better.
You were right.	I was wrong.
Maybe we could just start over.	I shouldn't have said that.

Spend time in prayer asking for God's help in improving the communication in your family.

Session 1: "Communicating"
Date

SESSION TWO

FAMILY ROLES AND GOALS

Key Verses

"Children, obey your parents in the Lord, for this is right. Fathers, do not exasperate your children; instead, bring them up in the training and instruction of the Lord."
Ephesians 6:1,4

Biblical Basis

Exodus 20:12;
Proverbs 10:1; 13:1; 15:5;
Matthew 10:37-39; 18:6,7;
Mark 10:43-45;
1 Corinthians 13:1-7,13;
Ephesians 6:1-4;
Philippians 2:3-5; 3:14; 4:19;
1 Timothy 5:8

The Big Idea

When biblical principles are implemented in the home, stronger, healthier relationships are developed.

Aims of This Session

During this session you will guide students to:
- Examine the various roles and goals of their families;
- Discover their part in creating successful family environments;
- Implement a plan to help their homes conform better to the biblical principles for families.

Warm Up

Family Coat of Arms—
Students draw coats of arms to represent their families.

Team Effort—Junior High/Middle School

God and Goals—
Students evaluate their goals in light of God's Word.

Team Effort—High School

Family Goals—
Students discuss their families' goals.

In the Word

What the Bible Says About Families—
A Bible study of verses relevant to family relationships.

Things to Think About (Optional)

Questions to get the students thinking and talking about God's plan for families.

Parent Page

A tool to get the session into the home and allow parents and young people to discuss their individual roles and their family goals.

SESSION TWO

FAMILY ROLES AND GOALS

LEADER'S DEVOTIONAL

"Whoever wants to become great among you must be your servant, and whoever wants to be first must be slave of all. For even the Son of Man did not come to be served, but to serve, and to give his life as a ransom for many" (Mark 10:43-45).

If you were to ask the students in your ministry, "What TV family most resembles your own?" what do you think they'd say? *Home Improvement? Full House? Married with Children? The Brady Bunch? The Simpsons?* Scary question! And I'm not sure we'd really want to know their responses.

Teaching teenagers what the Bible says about family roles and goals will be a new experience for most of your students. Why? Because most families don't talk about roles and goals. Instead of discussing how to develop family unity and implementing a number of the helpful ideas found in this lesson, most parents lean on the tried-and-not-so-true eye-rolling phrases teenagers hear all the time:

I'm the parent around here, and you'll do what I say!

If you don't like it here, you can pack your bags and leave!

Because I said so!

It'd be nice to think that family problems and conflict would be solved in 30 quick, easy, painless minutes like teenagers see every night on TV, but in this modern world of single-parent, divorced and blended families I'm not sure the quickest solution would be the best solution. (Especially if it's a TV solution!) Most teenagers don't even think about setting goals for the part they play in their families. And most parents don't do a very good job of defining what the various roles are in the family. For students who come from relatively good homes, this lesson will help them clarify and understand the important role they play in their families. For students who come from broken homes, it will give them the tools to be a positive influence in their families. For every student, this lesson will provide a biblical blueprint for implementing God's plan for families. This lesson is a great place for everyone to start their own home improvements. (Written by Joey O'Connor)

> "A happy family is but an earlier heaven."
> —John Bowring

SESSION TWO   BIBLE TUCK-IN™

FAMILY ROLES AND GOALS

Key Verses

"Children, obey your parents in the Lord, for this is right. Fathers, do not exasperate your children; instead, bring them up in the training and instruction of the Lord." Ephesians 6:1,4

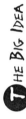 Biblical Basis

Exodus 20:12; Proverbs 10:1; 13:1; 15:5; Matthew 10:37-39; 18:6,7; Mark 10:43-45; 1 Corinthians 13:1-7,13; Ephesians 6:1-4; Philippians 2:3-5; 3:14; 4:19; 1 Timothy 5:8

The Big Idea

When biblical principles are implemented in the home, stronger, healthier relationships are developed.

Warm Up (5-10 Minutes)

Family Coat of Arms

- Give each student a copy of "Family Coat of Arms" on page 33 and a pencil.
- Have them draw or write a representation of each of the listed items in the area with the corresponding number.
- If time allows, have each student share his or her coat of arms with a partner.
  1. Family name
  2. Where the family is from
  3. Our family's favorite meal
  4. Our family's favorite tradition (e.g. eating Chinese food at Christmas)
  5. Something unique about our family
  6. Our favorite family activity
  7. Our favorite funniest event
  8. Draw a family portrait

31

Things to Think About (optional)

- Use the questions on page 38 after or as a part of "In the Word."
  1. What are several key principles that are a part of God's design for families?
  2. Why do families in our world struggle so much with carrying out God's principles for the family?
  3. How does Philippians 2:3-5 – "Do nothing out of selfish ambition or vain conceit, but in humility consider others better than yourselves. Each of you should look not only to your own interests, but also to the interests of others" – apply to families?

 Parent Page

- Distribute page to parents.

Team Effort—Junior High/Middle School (15-20 Minutes)

God and Goals

- Divide students into pairs.
- Give each student a copy of "God and Goals" on page 34 and a pen or pencil, or display a copy using an overhead projector.
- Have students finish the statements, then discuss the page with their partners.

"I press on toward the goal to win the prize for which God has called me heavenward in Christ Jesus" (Philippians 3:14).

Complete the following statements, then discuss your completions with your partner.

A goal for my relationship with my family is...
Before I die, I hope that...
A spiritual goal that I have for my life is...
The thing that may help me achieve this goal is...
The thing that could keep me from reaching this goal is...
My chances of reaching my goal are...

Team Effort—High School (15-20 Minutes)

Family Goals

- Divide students into groups of three or four.
- Give each student a copy of "Family Goals" on page 35 and a pen or pencil, or display a copy using an overhead projector.
- Have students complete the page individually and then discuss their answers with their small group members.

1. What areas of your home life need the most improvement?
2. What specific individual accomplishments do you want to make?
3. What goals would you like to set for your family?
4. What changes will have to be made to accomplish these goals?
5. What are the problems or hindrances in attaining these goals?
6. What is the divine promise in Philippians 4:19: "My God will meet all your needs according to his glorious riches in Christ Jesus"?

How does this promise relate to your family goals?

In The Word (25-30 Minutes)

What the Bible Says About Families

- Divide students into groups of three or four.
- Give each student a copy of "What the Bible Says About Families" on pages 36-37 and a pen or pencil.
- After each Bible reference, have group members write what that Scripture teaches about the family and what change should be made in their homes to better conform to these biblical principles. (The material in parenthesis is for the leader's reference only and does not appear on student pages.)

Biblical Families

Verse	Teaching	Change
Exodus 20:12	(Respect your parents.)	
Proverbs 10:1	(Act wisely.)	
Proverbs 13:1	(Follow your parents' instructions.)	
Proverbs 15:5	(Submit to parental discipline.)	
Matthew 10:37-39	(Put Christ first in your life.)	
Matthew 18:6,7	(Parents should not lead children into sin.)	
1 Corinthians 13:1-7,13	(Love each other.)	
Ephesians 6:1-4	(Children and parents should respect each other.)	
1 Timothy 5:8	(Parents should provide for the family.)	

So What?

Which of the biblical principles are the most evident in your family?

Which of the biblical principles does your family need to work on?

SESSION TWO

FAMILY ROLES AND GOALS

FAMILY COAT OF ARMS

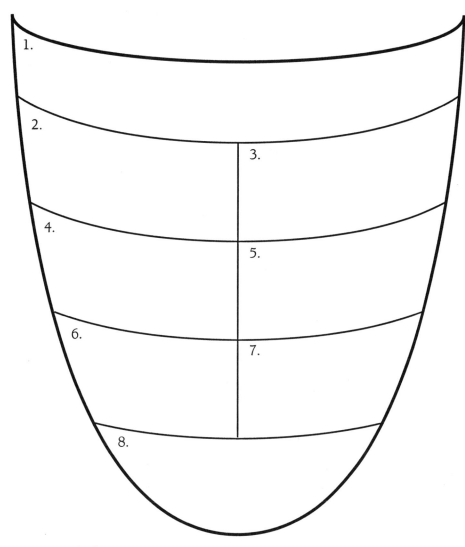

Draw or write the following in the corresponding numbered spaces:
1. Family name
2. Where the family is from
3. Our family's favorite meal
4. Our family's favorite tradition (e.g. eating Chinese food at Christmas)
5. Something unique about our family
6. Our favorite family activity
7. Our favorite funniest event
8. Draw a family portrait

© 1997 by Gospel Light. Permission to photocopy granted. *The Word on Family*

SESSION TWO

FAMILY ROLES AND GOALS

Team Effort

God and Goals

"I press on toward the goal to win the prize for which God has called me heavenward in Christ Jesus" (Philippians 3:14).

Complete the following statements, then discuss your completions with a partner.

A goal for my relationship with my family is...

....
....
....

Before I die, I hope that...

....
....
....

A spiritual goal that I have for my life is...

....
....
....

The thing that may help me achieve this goal is...

....
....
....

The thing that could keep me from reaching this goal is...

....
....
....

My chances of reaching my goal are...

....
....
....

SESSION TWO

Team Effort

Family Goals

1. What areas of your home life need the most improvement?

2. What specific individual accomplishments do you want to make?

3. What goals would you like to set for your family?

4. What changes will have to be made to accomplish these goals?

5. What are the problems or hindrances in attaining these goals?

6. What is the divine promise in Philippians 4:19: "My God will meet all your needs according to his glorious riches in Christ Jesus"?

   How does this promise relate to my family goals?

© 1997 by Gospel Light. Permission to photocopy granted. *The Word on Family*

SESSION TWO

FAMILY ROLES AND GOALS

IN THE WORD

WHAT THE BIBLE SAYS ABOUT FAMILIES

Verse	Teaching	Change
Exodus 20:12		
Proverbs 10:1		
Proverbs 13:1		
Proverbs 15:5		
Matthew 10:37-39		
Matthew 18:6,7		
1 Corinthians 13:1-7,13		

SESSION TWO

FAMILY ROLES AND GOALS

Verse	Teaching	Change
Ephesians 6:1-4		
	....	....
	....	....
	....	....
1 Timothy 5:8		
	....	....
	....	....
	....	....

So What?

Which of the biblical principles are the most evident in your family?

....
....
....

Which of the biblical principles does your family need to work on?

....
....
....

SESSION TWO

FAMILY ROLES AND GOALS

Things to Think About

1. What are several key principles that are a part of God's design for families?

   ....
   ....
   ....

2. Why do families in our world struggle so much with carrying out God's principles for the family?

   ....
   ....
   ....

3. How does Philippians 2:3-5 – "Do nothing out of selfish ambition or vain conceit, but in humility consider others better than yourselves. Each of you should look not only to your own interests, but also to the interests of others" – apply to families?

   ....
   ....
   ....

SESSION TWO

Parent Page

Family Roles and Goals

Read Psalm 37:4; Proverbs 16:3,4; Galatians 2:20; Colossians 3:17.

With these Scriptures in mind, describe to each other who you are. Describe your roles and goals.

Who Am I?

Example from Jim Burns's life:

Roles	Goals
Christian	Surrender my life to Jesus Christ and follow Him daily
Husband	Love my wife; court her; treat her with honor
Dad	Spend quality time; model Christianity to my children
President of NIYM	Lead ministry; seek to serve youth, youth workers and parents

Who Am I?

Roles	Goals
_____	_____
_____	_____
_____	_____
_____	_____
_____	_____

Session 2: "Family Roles and Goals"
Date ....

© 1997 by Gospel Light. Permission to photocopy granted. *The Word on Family*

SESSION THREE

EXPRESSING APPRECIATION

Key Verse

"Therefore encourage one another and build each other up, just as in fact you are doing." 1 Thessalonians 5:11

Biblical Basis

Proverbs 12:15; 15:31,32; 18:13; 1 Thessalonians 5:11,18; James 1:22-25

The Big Idea

Family members need to express words of encouragement to one another often.

Aims of This Session

During this session you will guide students to:
- Examine ways to show love and encouragement to their family members;
- Discover the biblical basis for expressing affirmation;
- Implement a strategy to create a family environment of listening, encouragement and affirmation.

Warm Up

Good Times—
Students reminisce about good times with their families.

Team Effort— Junior High/ Middle School

Thank Therapy—
Making a list of things to be thankful for.

Team Effort— High School

You're the Greatest!—
Students write a note of appreciation to their parents.

In the Word

Listening and Affirming—
A Bible study on how to encourage others.

Things to Think About (Optional)

Questions to get students thinking and talking about communicating appreciation to family members.

Parent Page

A tool to get the session into the home and allow parents and young people to discuss the different ways to express love.

SESSION THREE

EXPRESSING APPRECIATION

LEADER'S DEVOTIONAL

"Give thanks in all circumstances, for this is God's will for you in Christ Jesus" (1 Thessalonians 5:18).

Rock-climbing gyms, mountain biking, trekking adventures to Nepal, river rafting, Toyota 4-Runners, windsurfing, Nissan Pathfinders, military-converted civilian Hummers and in-your-face commercials showing every extreme sport known to mankind so far—the excesses of the '80s have transmogrified themselves to the environmentally friendly outdoor lifestyle of '90s ARPies, Affluent Recreating Professionals. They've traded in the Beamer for backcountry helicopter skiing and their stock options for a semi-spiritualized form of simplicity. Oh, and let's not forget about the gear—the stuff—and lots of it!

Swept right along this new riptide of environmental materialism are the teenagers in your youth group. Check out all the rock 'n' roll pounding Gen X commercials on TV and it's clear who's the target of the latest soft drink or sport utility vehicle. And if teenagers are the target for the product, can you guess who's targeted to pay for all this stuff? You've got it: the parents!

One of the most logical places to start helping teenagers express appreciation for their parents is to help young people understand what they do have (i.e. how their parents have provided for them). Too often, teenagers focus on what they don't have. As adults, we do the same thing. We'd like to have that steel blue Range Rover. We'd like to spend a week rafting the Grand Canyon. And in the process of wanting more stuff and attempting to define our lives by what we have, our hearts shrink as we lose the vision of who we are in Christ.

Gratefulness. Thankfulness. Contentment. Appreciation. Those are rich words that can fill a family with meaning and significance. They are words that can teach teenagers what truly matters. They are the kind of words that can make an amazing difference in your life today—and they're absolutely free! (Written by Joey O'Connor)

"The deepest principle in human nature is the craving to be appreciated."—William James

SESSION THREE   BIBLE TUCK-IN™

EXPRESSING APPRECIATION

EY VERSE

"Therefore encourage one another and build each other up, just as in fact you are doing."
1 Thessalonians 5:11

BIBLICAL BASIS

Proverbs 12:15; 15:31,32; 18:13; 1 Thessalonians 5:11,18; James 1:22-25

THE BIG IDEA

Family members need to express words of encouragement to one another often.

WARM UP (5-10 Minutes)

GOOD TIMES
- Give each student a copy of "Good Times" on page 45 and a pen or pencil, or display a copy using an overhead projector and give each student a piece of paper and a pen or pencil.
- Give students one to two minutes to complete the page and then have them share some of their answers with the whole group.

Complete the following sentences:
A special time in my family's life was....

What I most appreciate about my parents is....

One of my favorite funny memories is....

---- Fold ----

43

PARENT PAGE

- Distribute page to parents.

Team Effort—Junior High/Middle School (15-20 Minutes)

Thank Therapy

- Display a copy of "Thank Therapy" on page 46 using an overhead projector and give each student a piece of paper and a pen or pencil. (Or give each student a copy of "Thank Therapy" on page 46 and a pen or pencil.)
- Give students two minutes to complete their lists.
- Divide the students into groups of three or four and have them share their answers with their small groups.

Sometimes in the heat of the battles of family life we miss the opportunity to look at the positive. Take a few moments to practice "thank therapy." "Write down 10 things for which you are thankful about your family. Share your answers with your group and don't forget to share them with your family!

> "Give thanks in all circumstances, for this is God's will for you in Christ Jesus"
> (1 Thessalonians 5:18).

Team Effort—High School (15-20 Minutes)

You're the Greatest!

- Give each student a piece of note paper and an envelope.
- Have students write a note of appreciation to their parents (or another family member).
- Suggest that they put their notes in the envelopes and either give or mail them to their parents.

In The Word (25-30 Minutes)

Listening and Affirming

- Divide students into groups of three or four.
- Give each student a copy of "Listening and Affirming" on pages 47-48 and a pen or pencil, or display a copy using an overhead projector.
- Have students complete the study in their small groups.

One of the most effective ways to encourage your family members, or anyone for that matter, is to honor them by listening to them. Listening is truly the language of love. Read each principle, then read the accompanying Scripture. Discuss the biblical principles with your group.

1. Listening is a sign of wisdom.   Proverbs 12:15
2. Listening must be accompanied by action.   James 1:22-25
3. Listening is more important than speaking.   Proverbs 18:13
4. The wise listen when others correct them.   Proverbs 15:31,32

So What?

A Ministry of Encouragement

Having a ministry of encouragement in your family is easy. It often doesn't come naturally, but there is incredible power in an encouraging word. Here's what you can do to have a ministry of encouragement:

1. **Believe in your parents (or other family members).**
   What struggles are your parents going through where they need you to believe in them?

   What struggles are other family members going through where they need you to believe in them?

2. **Be liberal with your praise for your parents and other family members.**

   > "Therefore encourage one another and build each other up, just as in fact you are doing" (1 Thessalonians 5:11).
   >
   > Mark Twain once said, "I can live two months on one good compliment."

   What specific thing(s) can you compliment your parent(s) on this week?

   What specific thing(s) can you compliment other family members on this week?

3. **Be available when family members need you.**
   How can you be more available to your parents?

   What special thing can you do for them this week?

   How can you be more available to other family members?

   What special thing(s) can you do for them this week?

Things To Think About (optional)

- Use the questions on page 49 after or as a part of "In the Word."

1. What makes expressing appreciation to parents so difficult?

2. How do your parents express appreciation to you?

3. What are issues that block communication with your parents?

SESSION THREE

EXPRESSING APPRECIATION

Warm Up

Good Times

Complete the following sentences:

A special time in my family's life was...
....
....
....

What I most appreciate about my parents is...
....
....
....

One of my favorite funny memories is...
....
....
....

SESSION THREE

EXPRESSING APPRECIATION

Team Effort

Thank Therapy

"Give thanks in all circumstances, for this is God's will for you in Christ Jesus" (1 Thessalonians 5:18).

Sometimes in the heat of the battles of family life we miss the opportunity to look at the positive. Take a few moments to practice "thank therapy." Write down 10 things for which you are thankful about your family. Share your answers with the group and don't forget to share them with your family!

1.

2.

3.

4.

5.

6.

7.

8.

9.

10.

SESSION THREE

EXPRESSING APPRECIATION

LISTENING AND AFFIRMING

One of the most effective ways to encourage your family members, or anyone for that matter, is to honor them by listening to them. Listening is truly the language of love. Read each principle, then read the accompanying Scripture. Discuss the biblical principles with your group.

1. Listening is a sign of wisdom.   Proverbs 12:15
2. Listening must be accompanied by action.   James 1:22-25
3. Listening is more important than speaking.   Proverbs 18:13
4. The wise listen when others correct them.   Proverbs 15:31,32

So What?

A Ministry of Encouragement

Having a ministry of encouragement in your family is easy. It often doesn't come naturally, but there is incredible power in an encouraging word. Here's what you can do to have a ministry of encouragement:

1. Believe in your parents (or other family members).

What struggles are your parents going through where they need you to believe in them?

....
....
....

What struggles are other family members going through where they need you to believe in them?

....
....

2. Be liberal with your praise for your parents and other family members.

> "Therefore encourage one another and build each other up, just as in fact you are doing" (1 Thessalonians 5:11).

> Mark Twain once said, "I can live two months on one good compliment."

What specific thing(s) can you compliment your parent(s) on this week?

....
....
....

© 1997 by Gospel Light. Permission to photocopy granted. *The Word on Family*

SESSION THREE

EXPRESSING APPRECIATION

What specific thing(s) can you compliment other family members on this week?
....
....

3. Be available when family members need you.

How can you be more available to your parents?
....
....

What special thing can you do for them this week?
....
....
....

How can you be more available to other family members?
....
....

What special thing(s) can you do for them this week?
....
....
....

SESSION THREE

EXPRESSING APPRECIATION

Things to Think About

1. What makes expressing appreciation to parents so difficult?

2. How do your parents express appreciation to you?

3. What are issues that block communication with your parents?

SESSION THREE

EXPRESSING APPRECIATION

Parent Page

LEARNING A NEW LANGUAGE

We all express love in our own love language and we also appreciate love expressed toward us in that same language. In Gary Chapman's excellent book, *The Five Languages of Love*, he describes five different languages we use to express and accept love. They are:

- Words of Affirmation
- Quality Time
- Receiving Gifts
- Acts of Service
- Physical Touch

Have each family member answer the following questions:

1. Which of the above languages is your dominant "love language"?

2. Describe a time when another family member made you feel loved.

3. How can you be more sensitive to each others' needs?

Affirmation Bombardment

Take a few moments to affirm each member of your family. Write on a piece of paper three affirming comments about each person. Then one at a time have the others barrage each family member with words of affirmation.

Session 3: "Expressing Appreciation"
Date

SESSION FOUR

THE POWER OF BEING THERE

Key Verse

"He took the children in his arms, put his hands on them and blessed them." Mark 10:16

Biblical Basis

Mark 10:13-16;
Ephesians 4:22-24;
1 Thessalonians 2:8

The Big Idea

Family members regard your very presence as a sign of caring and connectedness.

Aims of This Session

During this session you will guide students to:
- Examine the powerful concept of the strength of "being there" for others;
- Discover how Jesus influenced people with a strong sense of His presence;
- Implement specific ways to be present in their families' lives.

Warm Up

Thanks for Being There—
Students remember how their parents have helped them.

Team Effort—Junior High/Middle School

Who's Influencing You?—
Students list those persons who have influenced them.

Team Effort—High School

The Power of Being There—
A story about how important someone's very presence in your life can be.

In the Word

The Blessings of Touch and Time—
A Bible study on the need to share in the lives of family members.

Things to Think About (Optional)

Questions to get students thinking and talking about giving time and attention to others.

Parent Page

A tool to get the session into the home and allow parents and young people to discuss the important people in their lives.

SESSION FOUR

THE POWER OF BEING THERE

LEADER'S DEVOTIONAL

"You were taught, with regard to your former way of life, to put off your old self, which is being corrupted by its deceitful desires; to be made new in the attitude of your minds; and to put on the new self, created to be like God in true righteousness and holiness" (Ephesians 4:22-24).

The Force is back. Can you believe it? After lying dormant in a distant galaxy for over fifteen years, the *Star Wars Trilogy* has skyrocketed back to the big screen. Luke Skywalker, Princess Leia, Han Solo, Chewbacca, R2-D2, C-3PO and that light-saber-swinging Darth Vader are all making a historical return to Planet Earth. With 15 million dollars, new scenes and 150 newly enhanced special effects, the new and improved *Star Wars* promises to make a big impact on a whole new generation of *Star Wars* fans.

Star Wars, The Empire Strikes Back, and *The Return of the Jedi*—these three science fiction movies have made a major cultural impact on America and on subsequent Hollywood blockbuster hits. Can the same be said about families today? Though the Force in *Star Wars* does some highly unusual and interesting things, there is not a more powerful force in families today than the power of presence. Being there by making yourself available to your family will impact the future generations of your family long after Luke Skywalker has blown apart the Death Star for the last time.

Not only does your presence have a powerful impact on your own family, being there for the students in your youth ministry is at the heart of working with young people. Every youth ministry has guys without dads, girls without moms, workaholic parents and dysfunctional families—that's what makes your positive influence so important. Even for students who come from less-than-ideal families, this lesson will help them understand how their presence can change their families for the better.

Never underestimate the power of your presence. Being there is the heart of the gospel. In Jesus Christ, God made Himself present to us despite our sin, our weakness and our shortcomings. In Christ, God is with us in human flesh. Just as you are with your students. (Written by Joey O'Connor)

> **"Many a son has lost his way among strangers because his father was too busy to get acquainted with him."**
> **—William L. Brownell**

SESSION FOUR

BIBLE TUCK-IN™

THE POWER OF BEING THERE

 KEY VERSE

"He took the children in his arms, put his hands on them and blessed them." Mark 10:16

 BIBLICAL BASIS

Mark 10:13-16; Ephesians 4:22-24; 1 Thessalonians 2:8

 THE BIG IDEA

Family members regard your very presence as a sign of caring and connectedness.

 WARM UP (5-10 MINUTES)

THANKS FOR BEING THERE
• Give each student a blank piece of paper and a pen or pencil.
• Ask everyone to take three minutes and write out as many things as possible that their parents and other family members have done for them this week.
• Then have each person share at least one thing his or her parents have done for them this past week.

THINGS TO THINK ABOUT (OPTIONAL)

• Use the questions on page 59 after or as a part of "In the Word."
1. Jesus often blessed people by touching them. Why do you think touch is such a powerful way to bless others?

2. Why do you think that giving your time and attention to people is the most powerful gift you can give them?

3. Who has been a person who has given you time, attention and affection? Have you thanked that person for his or her presence in your life?

 PARENT PAGE

• Distribute page to parents.

Team Effort—Junior High/Middle School (15-20 Minutes)

Who's Influencing You?

- Divide students into groups of three or four.
- Give each student a copy of "Who's Influencing You?" on page 55 and a pen or pencil, or display a copy using an overhead projector, and give each student a piece of paper and a pen or pencil.
- When students have completed their lists, have them each share one influential person and the reason why they chose that person.

Name the five most influential people in your life and tell how they have influenced you:

Name	Reason

Team Effort—High School (15-20 Minutes)

The Power of Being There

- Divide students into groups of three or four.
- Give each group a copy of "The Power of Being There" on page 56 and ask them to read the story aloud and then discuss the questions in their small groups.

1. Who has had the power-of-being-there-type of influence in your life? How is your life affected/influenced because of this person?
2. What is the best part of knowing that someone will be there for you?
3. Can you think of an illustration from the Bible where Christ had a power-of-being-there influence on someone?

In The Word (25-30 Minutes)

The Blessings of Touch and Time

- Divide students into groups of three or four.
- Give each student a copy of "The Blessings of Touch and Time" on pages 57-58 and a pen or pencil, or display a copy using an overhead projector.
- Have students complete the study in their small groups.

Read the following together aloud:

> "People were bringing little children to Jesus to have him touch them, but the disciples rebuked them. When Jesus saw this, he was indignant. He said to them, 'Let the little children come to me, and do not hinder them, for the kingdom of God belongs to such as these. I tell you the truth, anyone who will not receive the kingdom of God like a little child will never enter it.' And he took the children in his arms, put his hands on them and blessed them" (Mark 10:13-16).

There is a very special place in the heart of God for children and families.

Read Mark 10:13,14.
What did the disciples do when people brought little children to Jesus?
How did Jesus react to the disciples?
Why do you think Jesus allowed the little children to come to him?
How do the following quote and Scripture verse relate to the idea of blessing your family with your presence?

> "Family members regard your very presence as a sign of caring and connectedness."
> "We loved you so much that we were delighted to share with you not only the gospel of God but our lives as well, because you have become so dear to us" (1 Thessalonians 2:8).

What specifically can you do to bless your family with your presence?

Bless Your Family with Your Presence

"He took the children in his arms, put his hands on them and blessed them" (Mark 10:16).

How did Jesus bless the children?

UCLA researchers have found that it takes 8 to 10 meaningful touches a day for a person to feel loved. Many people are literally starved for physical attention, affection and warmth even though they are members of a family whose members do love one another.

Bless Your Family with Affection

On a scale from 1 to 10 how would you rate your family's ability to show affection?

```
Hug-O-Meter
1            5             10
We never     So-so         Extremely
show affection              affectionate
```

So What?

What are one or two things you can do this week to bless each family member with affection? (For example: bring Mom flowers, write an "I love you" or "I appreciate you" note, give a neck rub, hug family members without being asked, etc.) Think of something specific to do for each family member.

SESSION FOUR

THE POWER OF BEING THERE

Team Effort

Who's Influencing You?

Name the five most influential people in your life and tell how they have influenced you.

Name   **Reason**
_____   _____
_____   _____
_____   _____
_____   _____

SESSION FOUR

Team Effort

The Power of Being There

My Mom died a few years ago. It wasn't easy. Cancer racked her body and we spent most of a year watching her die.

We had moved Mom home from the hospital and we were trying to make her as comfortable as possible. We moved a hospital bed into Mom and Dad's bedroom. I would often find myself sitting on their bed while she lay in her hospital bed.

One day she was dozing and very weak, when all of a sudden she perked up and asked me, "Jimmy, where is your dad?"

"He's watching a ball game on TV. Do you need him, Mom?"

"No, not really," she replied. Then she looked up at me and said, "You know Jimmy, I never really liked baseball."

"You never liked baseball, Mom?" I was so very puzzled. "Did you ever miss a little league game of mine?"

"No."

"Did you ever miss any of my Pony league, junior high or high school games, Mom?"

Again she replied, "I don't think so."

"Mom," I continued, "you never missed a game and on top of that you never missed any of my three brothers' games either. Dad and you watch ball games all day long on TV. What do you mean you never liked baseball?"

"Jimmy, I didn't go to the games to watch baseball. I went to the games to be with you!"

I realized at that moment why this incredible woman had had such a powerful impact on my life because of the power of being there even when she didn't care for the activity. Her very presence in my life was cause for great inspiration and influence.

1. Who has had the power-of-being-there-type of influence in your life? How is your life affected/influenced because of this person?

   ....
   ....
   ....

2. What is the best part of knowing that someone will be there for you?

   ....
   ....
   ....

3. Can you think of an illustration from the Bible where Christ had a power-of-being-there influence on someone?

   ....
   ....
   ....

© 1997 by Gospel Light. Permission to photocopy granted. *The Word on Family*

SESSION FOUR

THE POWER OF
BEING THERE

In the Word

The Blessings of Touch and Time

Read the following together aloud:

> "People were bringing little children to Jesus to have him touch them, but the disciples rebuked them. When Jesus saw this, he was indignant. He said to them, 'Let the little children come to me, and do not hinder them, for the kingdom of god belongs to such as these. I tell you the truth, anyone who will not receive the kingdom of God like a little child will never enter it.' And he took the children in his arms, put his hands on them and blessed them" (Mark 10:13-16).

There is a very special place in the heart of God for children and families.

Bless Your Family with Your Presence

Read Mark 10:13,14.

What did the disciples do when people brought little children to Jesus?

How did Jesus react to the disciples?

Why do you think Jesus allowed the little children to come to him?

How do the following quote and Scripture relate to the idea of blessing your family with your presence?

> "Family members regard your very presence as a sign of caring and connectedness."

> "We loved you so much that we were delighted to share with you not only the gospel of God but our lives as well, because you have become so dear to us" (1 Thessalonians 2:8).

SESSION FOUR

THE POWER OF BEING THERE

What specifically can you do to bless your family with your presence?

....
....
....

Bless Your Family with Affection

"He took the children in his arms, put his hands on them and blessed them" (Mark 10:16).

How did Jesus bless the children?

....
....
....

UCLA researchers have found that it takes 8 to 10 meaningful touches a day for a person to feel loved. Many people are literally starved for physical attention, affection and warmth even though they are members of a family whose members do love one another.

Hug-O-Meter

On a scale from 1 to 10 how would you rate your family's ability to show affection?

1	5	10
We never show affection	So-so	Extremely affectionate

So What?

What are one or two things you can do this week to bless each family member with affection? (For example: bring Mom flowers, write an "I love you" or "I appreciate you" note, give a neck rub, hug family members without being asked, etc.) Think of something specific to do for each family member.

© 1997 by Gospel Light. Permission to photocopy granted. *The Word on Family*

SESSION FOUR

THE POWER OF BEING THERE

Things to Think About

1. Jesus often blessed people by touching them. Why do you think touch is such a powerful way to bless others?

   ....
   ....
   ....

2. Why do you think that giving your time and attention to people is the most powerful gift you can give them?

   ....
   ....
   ....

3. Who has been a person who has given you time, attention and affection? Have you thanked that person for his or her presence in your life?

   ....
   ....
   ....

SESSION FOUR

THE POWER OF BEING THERE

Parent Page

NENE

Nene was one of the major heroes of my life. At 87 she was definitely losing it physically and her mental condition had deteriorated because of a crummy disease she had called Alzheimer's. Sometimes she recognized me and sometimes she didn't. I never dreamed she would live to see our last child born, but she did. She was even able to come to the baby shower. I have a picture of Nene holding our youngest daughter, Heidi. Both have a dazed look on their faces. Nevertheless, I treasure that picture to this day.

When it was time to open the presents, my brother, Bill, went over to help Nene out of her chair. I happened to be walking by when he said, "Come on Nene, let's go watch Jim and Cathy open those baby shower presents for their new baby, Heidi."

Dazed and confused, she said, "Who?"

He said, "Jim and Cathy had a baby and we are going to open some gifts, come on I'll help you up."

Frustrated and in pain, she told Bill, "I can't get up. I didn't buy them a present. I'm tired, I'm old, I'm sick and I just want to die."

Bill replied, "Nene, I don't think anyone is concerned that you didn't get them a gift."

At this point I walked up to my dear, loving Grandma and said, "Nene, your very presence in this room makes a difference to me. For all my life just your presence has given me strength."

Nene died shortly after the baby shower. She never really had much money, but it was never her gifts that made a difference, it was her very presence that still gives me strength today.

Discuss the following questions with family members:

1. How is "being present" a gift to those you love?

5. How have you experienced God's presence in your family's life?

2. Who has been a source of strength by their mere presence in your life like Nene was to Jim?

3. How has that person made a difference to you?

4. What prevents you from "being there" for other family members?

Session 4: "The Power of Being There"
Date

© 1997 by Gospel Light. Permission to photocopy granted. *The Word on Family*

Unit II

RESPECT

LEADER'S PEP TALK

Like many of you, I grew up in a home where we did not attend church. My parents were good people, but the Christian faith was definitely not a priority in our home. I became a Christian at 16. My youth worker, John Watson, told us once in a Bible study that God gave us our parents. He quoted Psalm 139 and said God formed each one of us in our mothers' wombs. My first reaction was that there must have been a mistake because my parents did not attend church. Later on John helped me understand that my parents were a part of God's plan in my life and that he placed me with them for a good purpose. He told me that my job was to obey and honor them and that God would bless me.

As a high school student, I'm not sure I ever really believed my youth worker's advice. However, today many, many years later I couldn't agree with him more. Although I didn't always obey and honor them like I should have, I do believe that God put my two very special parents in my life and me in their lives for a reason.

Some of the kids you are working with in your youth group don't like their parents right now. While some have great Christian role models, others are torn down from the moment they walk in the doors of their homes. One of the key messages of this section is that regardless of their experience, God has placed their parents in their lives for a reason, and it's time for the students to take on some of the responsibility for helping their families succeed.

SESSION FIVE

HONOR AND OBEY

Key Verse

"'Honor your father and your mother, so that you may live long in the land the LORD your God is giving you.'" Exodus 20:12

Biblical Basis

Exodus 20:12;
Psalm 139:13-16;
Ephesians 6:1-3;
Colossians 3:20

The Big Idea

God's command is to honor and obey our parents. Obeying His command will be rewarded.

Aims of This Session

During this session you will guide students to:
- Examine the biblical commandment to honor and obey their parents;
- Discover what God's plan is for a parent and child relationship;
- Implement a specific plan to honor and obey their parents.

Warm Up

Parents' Famous Sayings—

Students race to complete common statements parents make.

Team Effort— Junior High/ Middle School

Honoring and Obeying—

Students discuss what it means to honor their parents.

Team Effort— High School

George: A Case Study—

Discussion on students' responsibilities to parents.

In the Word

God's Gift—

A Bible study examining what it means to honor and obey parents.

Things to Think About (Optional)

Questions to get students thinking and talking about why God wants them to obey their parents.

Parent Page

A tool to get the session into the home and allow parents and young people to discuss the appropriateness of their family rules.

SESSION FIVE

HONOR AND OBEY

Leader's Devotional

"Listen, my son, to your father's instruction and do not forsake your mother's teaching" (Proverbs 1:8).

On October 12, 1996, Mike Cito, center for Albuquerque's St. Pius X High School football team, wore a razor-sharp helmet buckle during a football game that caused serious injuries to five opponents on the Albuquerque Academy's team. During the criminal trial that ensued as a result of the injuries, when questioned by the presiding judge, Cito admitted that his father, who is a children's dentist, was the one who sharpened the buckle. Both father and son were charged with conspiracy to commit aggravated assault and were sentenced to community service and probation. When asked why the buckle was sharpened, Mike Cito replied, "It was sharpened to protect me from harm."

It is shocking to consider what some parents will do today to help their kids have an edge over others. Wearing a sharpened helmet buckle at a father's request isn't what God had in mind when it comes to honoring and obeying parents. Mike Cito's misguided reasoning for wearing a sharpened buckle to protect himself from harm distorts the spiritual truth: Honoring and obeying parents always begins with obeying God, and He promised to reward our obedience.

Honor and obey. By honoring and obeying God not only do you benefit by experiencing His peace and presence in your life, but you also save yourself from the pain of poor choices, regrets and negative consequences. Sin, like a sharpened buckle, not only hurts God and those we sin against, but it also cuts deep into our hearts, separating us from the One who died for us.

Honoring and obeying parents may be number 1,381,024 on the list of topics your youth group wants to discuss. Yes, you're bound to hear ear-piercing shrieks of students wailing, "But you don't live with my parents!" Don't be discouraged and don't be afraid—this is a rewarding lesson that outlives the many benefits teenagers gain by honoring and obeying their folks. Besides, they've grown up with the playground maxim: Play by the rules and nobody will get hurt. (Written by Joey O'Connor)

> "It is better to deserve honors and not have them than to have them and not deserve them."—Mark Twain

SESSION FIVE   BIBLE TUCK-IN™

HONOR AND OBEY

KEY VERSE

"Honor your father and your mother, so that you may live long in the land the LORD your God is giving you." Exodus 20:12

BIBLICAL BASIS

Exodus 20:12; Psalm 139:13-16; Ephesians 6:1-3; Colossians 3:20

THE BIG IDEA

God's command is to honor and obey our parents. Obeying His command will be rewarded.

WARM UP (5-10 MINUTES)

PARENTS' FAMOUS SAYINGS
- Divide class into teams with fairly even numbers of students on each team.
- Give each team a copy of "Parents' Famous Sayings" on page 67 and a pen or pencil.
- Have them race to see who can complete their papers the fastest.
- Option: Have the teams come up with the funniest, most creative or outrageous completions to the sentences (e.g., Did you brush your ___nose___?)

If I've told you once, I've told you _____.
I don't know, go ask your _____.
Did you flush the _____?
Did you turn off the _____?
Shut the door. Were you born in a _____?
Don't talk with your mouth _____.
Don't eat that now. It will spoil your _____.
Did you brush your _____?
It's cold. Don't forget to take a _____.

---- Fold ----

YOUR RESPONSE
The Bible challenges us to honor and obey our parents. God's Word is very clear about how we should treat our parents. Read the following verses and answer the questions:
Colossians 3:20: What is well pleasing to the Lord?

Exodus 20:12 (one of the Ten Commandments): What is the promise at the end of this verse?

How do you think this promise relates to obeying your parents?

Ephesians 6:1-3: What are the results of honoring and obeying your parents?

SO WHAT?
Brainstorm, then list specific ways you can honor your parents in each of the following areas:

Respect

Encouragement

Affection

Attitude

THINGS TO THINK ABOUT (OPTIONAL)
- Use the questions on page 72 after or as a part of "In the Word."
1. What's the most difficult part of honoring and obeying your parents?

2. Why do you think God included honoring your parents as one of the Ten Commandments?

3. What if your parents ask you to do something that goes against the Bible's teachings? How can you honor God and yet honor your parents at the same time?

PARENT PAGE
- Distribute page to parents.

65

Now write down three of your own most often heard parent sayings.

1.
2.
3.

Team Effort—Junior High/Middle School (15-20 Minutes)

Honoring and Obeying

- Have students form pairs. Give each pair a copy of "Honoring and Obeying" on page 68 and a pen or pencil.
- Have them complete the page together.
- If there is time, discuss some of their responses with the whole group.

1. Your mother has a tendency toward smothering and nagging. Her concerns are almost always good and right, yet sometimes she can drive you crazy. Her major issues center around homework and the telephone. You are home alone doing your homework and the phone rings. It's your best friend and you talk on the phone for most of the afternoon. Your mother never finds out. Which statement best fits your opinion?

   A. I was wrong.
   B. It's no big deal.
   C. I was wrong, but it's no big deal.
   D. I should tell my Mom.
   E. This was just a little thing, but I would need to obey for something more important.

2. Your Dad has told you never to touch the beer he keeps in the cupboard. One day, while he is gone, your friends talk you into "borrowing" two cans of beer to just try the taste. You and your friends drink the beer. The next day your Dad specifically asks you if you took any of the beer from the cupboard. What do you do?

   A. You admit the deed and suffer the consequences.
   B. You lie and tell him you have no idea what happened to his beer.
   C. You tell him if he didn't want you to experiment with beer, he shouldn't have the beer around the house.
   D. You tell him that you are afraid your friends drank some beer, but you didn't touch the stuff.

3. Your parents are usually very honest people, but you know they cheat in their business. At the end of each night they close out the cash register early and basically keep two sets of financial books—one for the IRS and the other for them. This means they cheat on thousands of dollars of income taxes. What will you do?

   A. Confront them.
   B. Pray for them, but don't say anything.
   C. Call the IRS and report them.
   D. Other _____.

4. Now this situation changes a bit. In the summer you work part-time at your parents' business. They ask you to close out the register early every night. They tell you, "It's okay. Everybody else keeps two sets of books." Now what will you do?

   A. Tell them that based on your principles you can't do it.
   B. Honor and obey them.
   C. Call the police.
   D. Other _____.

---- Fold ----

Team Effort—High School (15-20 Minutes)

George: A Case Study

- Divide students into groups of three or four.
- Give each group a copy of "George: A Case Study" on page 69 or display a copy using an overhead projector.
- Have the groups read the case study and discuss the questions.

Some Sundays George wants to sleep in and miss church. Sometimes he would like to ditch the church youth group and not go to every activity. But his parents insist, "As long as you live in our house, you have to attend church." George's parents center their lives around church activities. They teach Bible classes and serve on church leadership committees. George loves his folks, respects their faith and is a Christian himself, but he doesn't want to be as "fanatical" as they are.

1. Do you think George's parents have the right to force church attendance on him? Why or why not?
2. If you were the pastor, what advice would you give to George? To his parents?
3. As a Christian, should George be more excited about his church involvement?
4. How could he become more enthusiastic?

In The Word (25-30 Minutes)

God's Gift

- Divide students into groups of three or four.
- Give each student a copy of "God's Gift" on pages 70-71 and a pen or pencil, or display a copy using an overhead projector.
- Have students complete the study in their small groups.

God Gave You Your Parents!

The first miracle of your life was that God gave you your parents! How do you feel about the above statement?

A. Thrilled
B. Thankful
C. Resentful
D. Wish I could trade them in on a new model
E. Other _____

How does Psalm 139:13-16 relate to the statement that God gave you your parents?

List five ways your parents have helped you become who you are today.

1.
2.
3.
4.
5.

SESSION FIVE

HONOR AND OBEY

Warm Up

Parents' Famous Sayings

If I've told you once, I've told you _____.
I don't know, go ask your _____.
Did you flush the _____?
Did you turn off the _____?
Shut the door. Were you born in a _____?
Don't talk with your mouth _____.
Don't eat that now. It will spoil your _____.
Did you brush your _____?
It's cold. Don't forget to take a _____.

Now write down three of your own most often heard parent sayings.

1. _____
2. _____
3. _____

SESSION FIVE

HONOR AND OBEY

Team Effort

HONORING AND OBEYING

1. Your mother has a tendency toward smothering and nagging. Her concerns are almost always good and right, yet sometimes she can drive you crazy. Her major issues center around homework and the telephone.

You are home alone doing your homework and the phone rings. It's your best friend and you talk on the phone for most of the afternoon. Your mother never finds out. Which statement best fits your opinion?
   A. I was wrong.
   B. It's no big deal.
   C. I was wrong but it's no big deal.
   D. I should tell my Mom.
   E. This was just a little thing but I would need to obey for something more important.

2. Your Dad has told you never to touch the beer he keeps in the cupboard. One day while he is gone, your friends talk you into "borrowing" two cans of beer to just try the taste. You and your friends drink the beer. The next day your Dad specifically asks you if you took any of the beer from the cupboard. What do you do?
   A. You admit the deed and suffer the consequences.
   B. You lie and tell him you have no idea what happened to his beer.
   C. You tell him if he didn't want you to experiment with beer, he shouldn't have the beer around the house.
   D. You tell him that you are afraid your friends drank some beer, but you didn't touch the stuff.

3. Your parents are usually very honest people but you know they cheat in their business. At the end of each night they close out the cash register early and basically keep two sets of financial books—one for the IRS and the other for them. This means they cheat on thousands of dollars of income taxes. What will you do?
   A. Confront them.
   B. Pray for them, but don't say anything.
   C. Call the IRS and report them.
   D. Other:_____

4. Now the situation changes a bit. In the summer you work part-time at your parents' business. They ask you to close out the register early every night. They tell you, "It's okay. Everybody else keeps two sets of books." Now what do you do?
   A. Tell them that based on your principles you can't do it.
   B. Honor and obey them.
   C. Call the police.
   D. Other:_____

© 1997 by Gospel Light. Permission to photocopy granted. *The Word on Family*

SESSION FIVE

HONOR AND OBEY

Team Effort

GEORGE: A CASE STUDY

George's parents center their lives around church activities. They teach Bible classes and serve on church leadership committees. George loves his folks, respects their faith and is a Christian himself, but he doesn't want to be as "fanatical" as they are.

Some Sundays George wants to sleep in and miss church. Sometimes he would like to ditch the church youth group and not go to every activity. But his parents insist, "As long as you live in our house, you have to attend church." George isn't opposed to going to church, but he is getting very frustrated at the amount of time he has to spend being involved.

1. Do you think George's parents have the right to force church attendance on him? Why or why not?

2. If you were the pastor, what advice would you give to George? To his parents?

3. As a Christian, should George be more excited about his church involvement?

4. How could he become more enthusiastic?

© 1997 by Gospel Light. Permission to photocopy granted. *The Word on Family*

SESSION FIVE

HONOR AND OBEY

 IN THE WORD

GOD'S GIFT

God Gave You Your Parents!
The first miracle of your life was that God specifically gave you your parents!
How do you feel about the above statement?
   A. Thrilled
   B. Thankful
   C. Resentful
   D. Wish I could trade them in on a new model
   E. Other _____

How does Psalm 139:13-16 relate to the statement that God gave you your parents?
....
....
....

List five ways your parents have helped you become who you are today.
   1.
   2.
   3.
   4.
   5.

Your Response
The Bible challenges us to honor and obey our parents. God's Word is very clear about how we should treat our parents. Read the following verses and answer the questions:

Colossians 3:20: What is well pleasing to the Lord?
....
....
....

Exodus 20:12 (one of the Ten Commandments): What is the promise at the end of this verse?
....
....
....

How do you think this promise relates to obeying your parents?
....
....
....

© 1997 by Gospel Light. Permission to photocopy granted. *The Word on Family*

SESSION FIVE

 HONOR AND OBEY

Ephesians 6:1-3: What are the results of honoring and obeying your parents?

....
....
....

So What?
Brainstorm, then list several specific ways you can honor your parents in each of the following areas.

Obedience

....
....
....

Respect

....
....
....

Encouragement

....
....
....

Affection

....
....
....

Attitude

....
....
....

SESSION FIVE

HONOR AND OBEY

Things to Think About

1. What's the most difficult part of honoring and obeying your parents?

2. Why do you think God included honoring your parents as one of the Ten Commandments?

3. What if your parents ask you to do something that goes against the Bible's teachings? How can you honor God and yet honor your parents at the same time?

SESSION FIVE

HONOR AND OBEY

Our Family Rules

Every family has rules to live by. Sometimes the rules are clear and easy to follow. Other times they seem a bit unfair. As a family, discuss your family rules using the following list of topics. Have each family member rate how they feel about each rule, using the following scale:

1. Absolutely fair
2. I can live with it, but...
3. Absolutely unfair
4. We don't have a rule for this one in our home.

Parent	Student	Topic	New Rule
___	___	clothing I wear	_____
___	___	television programs	_____
___	___	television time limits	_____
___	___	music I listen to	_____
___	___	allowance	_____
___	___	how I clean my room	_____
___	___	phone time	_____
___	___	curfew	_____
___	___	hairstyle	_____
___	___	chores	_____
___	___	bedtime	_____
___	___	movies I can see	_____

For each rule you rate a 3 (absolutely unfair), write a rule you think would be a more reasonable one. For each rule you rate a 4 write a rule that you can agree on.

Session 5: "Honor and Obey"
Date...........................

SESSION SIX

WALKING IN YOUR PARENTS' SHOES

Key Verses

"Near the cross of Jesus stood his mother, his mother's sister, Mary the wife of Clopas, and Mary Magdalene. When Jesus saw his mother there, and the disciple whom he loved standing nearby, he said to his mother, 'Dear woman, here is your son,' and to the disciple, 'Here is your mother.' From that time on, this disciple took her into his home." John 19:25-27

Biblical Basis

John 19:25-27;
Philippians 2:14

The Big Idea

In order to have healthy relationships with our parents, we sometimes need to understand why they act the way they do.

Aims of This Session

During this session you will guide students to:
- Examine the issues going on in their parents' lives;
- Discover how they can understand their parents' lives better;
- Implement a plan to help lighten their parents' load.

Warm Up

The Parent Quiz—
Students discover resemblances between themselves and their parents.

Team Effort—Junior High/Middle School

My Family, My Home—
Students consider the unique aspects of their own families.

Team Effort—High School

Let Me Introduce You—
Students share what they know about their parents.

In the Word

Walking in Your Parents' Shoes—
A Bible study examining the problems and pressures parents encounter.

Things to Think About (Optional)

Questions to get students thinking and talking about how to help and appreciate their parents.

Parent Page

A tool to get the session into the home and allow parents and young people to discover how they can help one another be more understanding.

SESSION SIX

WALKING IN YOUR PARENTS' SHOES

LEADER'S DEVOTIONAL

"Do everything without complaining or arguing" (Philippians 2:14).
When you were growing up, how often did your parents say to you:

Someday, when you're older, you'll understand.

This hurts me more than it hurts you.

When I was a kid, I used to walk ten miles to school in three feet of snow holding a warm potato in my freezing cold hands, and then I ate the potato for lunch!

Just wait until you're a parent someday!

And now—if you have kids of your own—how often do you say the same things? What goes around, comes around. Walking in our parents' shoes is never an easy task as an adult or a teenager. Teenagers just don't get it. They can't. That's what makes them teenagers. You, on the other hand, now know a little bit about what your parents were talking about. Trying to keep a family together—bills, finances, identity issues, career moves, responsibilities, in-laws. Someday, teenagers will understand—hopefully!

What I find wonderfully comforting in pondering the transition from adolescence to adulthood is that more than anyone else, Jesus knows what it's like to walk in another's shoes. He knows what it's like to walk in your shoes, your parents' shoes and the shoes of the teenagers you work with. Jesus is intimately acquainted with all of our ways. He even knows our shoe size.

Though most parents find it hard to relate to Generation-X teenagers, this lesson will aid teenagers in relating better to their parents. It will give them a chance to slip on their parents' shoes and walk with a new perspective on life. If we're willing to walk in another's shoes, those shoes will always fit. (Written by Joey O'Connor)

> "He who is carried on another's back does not appreciate how far the town is."
> —African proverb

SESSION SIX

BIBLE TUCK-IN™

WALKING IN YOUR PARENTS' SHOES

Key Verses

"Near the cross of Jesus stood his mother, his mother's sister, Mary the wife of Clopas, and Mary Magdalene. When Jesus saw his mother there, and the disciple whom he loved standing nearby, he said to his mother, 'Dear woman, here is your son,' and to the disciple, 'Here is your mother.' From that time on, this disciple took her into his home." John 19:25-27

Biblical Basis

John 19:25-27; Philippians 2:14

The Big Idea

In order to have healthy relationships with our parents, we sometimes need to understand why they act the way they do.

Warm Up (5-10 Minutes)

The Parent Quiz
- Divide students into groups of three or four.
- Give each student a copy of "The Parent Quiz" on page 79 and a pen or pencil.
- Give students two minutes to complete the quiz, then have them share their answers with their small groups.

	Mom	Dad
My personality is more like...	☐	☐
I look most like...	☐	☐
My faith is more like...	☐	☐
When I grow up, I'll probably be more like...	☐	☐
My communication style is more like my...	☐	☐
If I could spend one day alone with Mom or Dad, I would like to...		

Can you tell your parents that you need more guidance in certain areas? Why or why not?

4. Parents are often going through their own identity crises.
Just like the teenage years of identity crisis, your parents are probably having an identity crisis of their own. Parents are often worried about their jobs, their looks, their health, the future, finances, their relationships and their own parents (your grandparents)!
List three possible identity-crisis situations your parents may be going through right now.
1.
2.
3.

So What?

Given the reality of why your parents act the way they do, what can you specifically do to lighten their load?

Action	When/How Often?
Example: Help with the dishes	*Four times a week*

Things to Think About (optional)

- Use the questions on page 85 after or as a part of "In the Word."
1. My parents' biggest problem right now is...

2. I could be more helpful in our home if...

3. My happiest times with my family are when...

Parent Page

- Distribute page to parents.

Team Effort—Junior High/Middle School (15-20 Minutes)

My Family, My Home

- Give each student a copy of "My Family, My Home" on page 80 and a pen or pencil.
- Have students complete their papers by themselves.
- If time allows, have volunteers share at least one of their responses with the whole group.

Team Effort—High School (15-20 Minutes)

Let Me Introduce You

- Divide students into groups of three or four.
- Give each student a copy of "Let Me Introduce You" on page 81 and a pen or pencil.
- Give students two to three minutes to complete the following sentences.
- Have each student describe a family member to his or her small group. Encourage students to describe one of their parents, but allow them to choose another family member if they want to.

1. I would like to introduce you to a member of my family.

   This is my _____, _____.
                  (relationship)   (name)

   He/she is from _____.
   He/she is interested in _____.
   His/her heroes are _____.
   His/her occupation is _____.
   He/she has problems with _____.
   One of his/her greatest joys is _____.

2. The family activity I most enjoy is _____ because...

3. One thing I would change about my family to make it better, is...

In The Word (25-30 Minutes)

Walking in Your Parents' Shoes

- Divide students into a copy of three or four.
- Give each student a copy of "Walking in Your Parents' Shoes" on pages 82-84 and a pen or pencil, or display a copy using an overhead projector.
- Have students complete the study in their small groups.

Read John 19:25-27.

1. According to these verses in John, what duty did Jesus take care of before He died on the cross?

2. What was so special about His statement to His mother?

3. How did He demonstrate that He was "walking in his mother's shoes" even at the end of His life?

Fold

---

4. In what ways can you "walk" in your parents' shoes?

5. How would you rate your parents' lives? Place a mark by the word that best describes their lives.

   Dad
   ☐ Easy
   ☐ So-So
   ☐ Difficult

   Mom
   ☐ Easy
   ☐ So-So
   ☐ Difficult

Beginning to Understand Their Lives

Be fair to your parents. You will need to understand their pressures in order to understand why they are the way they are.

1. What kind of home lives did your parents grow up in? (If you don't know, plan to ask them.)

2. What problems and pressures are your parents having right now?

3. How are these problems affecting their relationship with you?

4. What can you do to help your parents?

Why Do They Act the Way They Do?

1. Nobody sent them to parenting school.
   You are probably their first family. Sure, they were raised in a family, but there is a major difference between being a kid in a family and being a mom or dad. Parenting is a difficult job so your parents are constantly in the process of trying to figure it out.
   If you could give your parents some advice on parenting, what would it be?

2. Your parents are possibly running a little scared.
   Your parents may never tell you this directly, but they are probably a little scared when it comes to raising you. They were teenagers once and they know how easy it is to blow it, and they probably understand some of the pressures in your life.
   How would you rank your parents on the following Overprotective Scale?

   1   10
   I'd like a few boundaries and I get none.   They smother me.

3. Parents are in the protection business.
   Parents often express their care and concern in overprotective ways. The best advice is to be patient and earn their trust.
   What are specific things you can do to earn the trust of your parents?

   What holds you back?

   Some parents aren't protective enough. What kinds of guidance would you like your parents to give you?

78

SESSION SIX

WALKING IN YOUR PARENTS' SHOES

Warm Up

The Parent Quiz

	Mom	Dad
My personality is more like...	☐	☐
I look most like...	☐	☐
My faith is more like...	☐	☐
When I grow up, I'll probably be more like...	☐	☐
My communication style is more like my...	☐	☐

If I could spend one day alone with Mom or Dad, I would like to...

SESSION SIX

WALKING IN YOUR PARENTS' SHOES

Team Effort

My Family, My Home

*A house is made of wood and stone;
A home is made of love alone.*

- What I count on the most from my family is
- One goal I would like our family to reach is to _____
- The biggest change in my family this past year was
- Our family changed a lot when
- One way our family could be more together is
- The family member I am concerned about the most is
- What means the most to me about my family is
- The most difficult thing for me to do with my family is _____
- When I'm alone in our home, I _____
- My main contribution to my family is
- Three words that best describe my family are
  1. ____
  2. ____
  3. ____
- My family is

© 1997 by Gospel Light. Permission to photocopy granted. *The Word on Family*

SESSION SIX

Team Effort

WALKING IN YOUR PARENTS' SHOES

Let Me Introduce You

1. I would like to introduce you to a member of my family.

   This is my _____, _____.
   　　　　　　　(relationship)　　　　　　　　(name)

   He/she is from _____.
   He/she is interested in _____.
   His/her heroes are _____.
   His/her occupation is _____.
   He/she has problems with _____.
   One of his/her greatest joys is _____.

2. The family activity I most enjoy is _____
   because...

   ....
   ....
   ....

3. One thing I would change about my family to make it better, is...

   ....
   ....
   ....

SESSION SIX

WALKING IN YOUR PARENTS' SHOES

IN THE WORD

WALKING IN YOUR PARENTS' SHOES
Read John 19:25-27.

1. According to these verses in John, what duty did Jesus take care of before He died on the cross?

2. What was so special about His statement to His mother?

3. How did He demonstrate that He was "walking in his mother's shoes" even at the end of His life?

4. In what ways can you "walk" in your parents' shoes?

5. How would you rate your parents' lives? Place a mark by the word that best describes their lives.

Dad	Mom
❑ Easy	❑ Easy
❑ So-So	❑ So-So
❑ Difficult	❑ Difficult

Beginning to Understand Their Lives
Be fair to your parents. You will need to understand their pressures in order to understand why they are the way they are.

1. What kind of home lives did your parents grow up in? (If you don't know, plan to ask them.)

© 1997 by Gospel Light. Permission to photocopy granted. *The Word on Family*

SESSION SIX

WALKING IN YOUR PARENTS' SHOES

2. What problems and pressures are your parents having right now?

....
....
....

3. How are these problems affecting their relationship with you?

....
....
....

4. What can you do to help your parents?

....
....
....

Why Do They Act the Way They Do?

1. Nobody sent them to parenting school.
   You are probably their first family. Sure, they were raised in a family, but there is a major difference between being a kid in a family and being a mom or dad. Parenting is a difficult job so your parents are constantly in the process of trying to figure it out.

   If you could give your parents some advice on parenting, what would it be?

2. Your parents are possibly running a little scared.
   Your parents may never tell you this directly, but they are probably a little scared when it comes to raising you. They were teenagers once and they know how easy it is to blow it, and they probably understand some of the pressures in your life.
   How would you rank your parents on the following Overprotective Scale?

   10_____1
   They smother me.   I'd like a few boundaries
                                                       and I get none.

3. Parents are in the protection business.
   Parents often express their care and concern in overprotective ways. The best advice is to be patient and earn their trust.

© 1997 by Gospel Light. Permission to photocopy granted. *The Word on Family*

SESSION SIX

WALKING IN YOUR PARENTS' SHOES

What are specific things you can do to earn the trust of your parents?

....
....
....

What holds you back?

....
....
....

Some parents aren't protective enough. What kinds of guidance would you like your parents to give you?

....
....
....

Can you tell your parents that you need more guidance in certain areas? Why or why not?

....
....

4. Parents are often going through their own identity crises.
   Just like the teenage years of identity crisis, your parents are probably having an identity crisis of their own. Parents are often worried about their jobs, their looks, their health, the future, finances, their relationships and their own parents (your grandparents)!
   List three possible identity-crisis situations your parents may be going through right now.
   1.
   2.
   3.

So What?

Given the reality of why your parents act the way they do, what can you specifically do to lighten their load?

Action	**When/How Often?**
Example: Help with the dishes	*Four times a week*
_____	_____
_____	_____
_____	_____
_____	_____

© 1997 by Gospel Light. Permission to photocopy granted. *The Word on Family*

SESSION SIX

WALKING IN YOUR PARENTS' SHOES

Things to Think About

1. My parents' biggest problem right now is...
   ....
   ....
   ....

2. I could be more helpful in our home if I...
   ....
   ....
   ....

3. My happiest times with my family are when...
   ....
   ....
   ....

SESSION SIX

WALKING IN YOUR PARENTS' SHOES

Parent Page

Parent Survey

Parents share your answers to the following with your son or daughter:

1. I would say my childhood was…
   - ❏ wonderful
   - ❏ good
   - ❏ okay
   - ❏ not so hot

   because…

   ....
   ....

2. When you were born, my deepest concern was…

   ....
   ....

3. My biggest problem or pressure right now is…

   ....
   ....

Questions for Students to Ask Parents

1. What can I do to be more helpful or to serve you more?

   ....
   ....

2. What are three areas of your life you would like me to pray about for you?

   ....
   ....

Questions for Parents to Ask Students

1. What can I do to be more sensitive to your needs and pressures?

   ....
   ....

2. What suggestions would you give to help make our family a better environment?

   ....
   ....

3. What are three areas of your life that I can be praying about for you?

   ....
   ....

Session 6: "Walking in Your Parents' Shoes"
Date ....

SESSION SEVEN

A TRIBUTE TO MOM

Key Verses

"A wife of noble character who can find? She is worth far more than rubies. Her children arise and call her blessed; her husband also, and he praises her." Proverbs 31:10,28

Biblical Basis

Proverbs 23:25; 31:10-31

The Big Idea

Your mom is a gift from God. She is to be affirmed and honored.

Aims of This Session

During this session you will guide students to:
- Examine the many ways our mothers care for us;
- Discover how we can appreciate and care for our mothers;
- Implement a biblical understanding of how and why we should pay tribute to our mothers.

Warm Up

The Mom Survey—
A group survey to discover unique moms.

Team Effort— Junior High/ Middle School

Mother Questionnaire—
Students discuss their feelings and memories about their mothers.

Team Effort— High School

Mom Reactions—
Students discuss how their mothers would react in certain situations.

In the Word

Locate the Trait—
A Bible study examining the godly woman described in Proverbs 31:10-31.

Things to Think About (Optional)

Questions to get students thinking and talking about mothers' duties and needs.

Parent Page

A tool to get the session into the home and allow moms and young people to interview one another.

SESSION SEVEN

A TRIBUTE TO MOM

LEADER'S DEVOTIONAL

"May your father and mother be glad; may she who gave you birth rejoice!" (Proverbs 23:25).

The Bible doesn't tell us much about Jesus' mom, Mary. What was it like raising a teenaged Messiah? What did Mary *really* say when Jesus stayed behind for a few days in Jerusalem when he was twelve years old? (If I had pulled a stunt like that, my mom would have skinned me alive!)

Did Mary have to nag Jesus about finishing his chores? Did she ever say to him, "You're NOT leaving this house dressed like that!" Did she ever question his choice of friends? (We certainly know that the Pharisees did years later.) Did Mary wander around the house picking up after Jesus?

Though the New Testament provides us with only a few snapshots of the life of Mary, she is the only person in the Gospels who experienced and witnessed the life of Christ from the cradle to the cross. Throughout the Gospels not only do we have glimpses of Mary's devotion and love to her son, but also her love and devotion to her God. In Mary, we see a faithful mother, a loving mother, a tender mother, a compassionate mother, and yes, a suffering mother. Whether yielding to the voice of God from an angel, searching for her missing young son, intervening on behalf of an embarrassed bride and groom or weeping bitterly at the foot of the cross, we have a consistent picture of the quality and character of this woman.

Just like we have a lot to learn from ministry mentors or other spiritual leaders we admire, the life of Mary shows us important character qualities that can make a difference in our lives today. Her devotion to God and her family not only impacted history, but also future generations. Being a mom today isn't easy, but neither was being the mom of the teenaged Messiah. (Written by Joey O'Connor)

> "All that I am or hope to be, I owe to my angel mother."
> —Abraham Lincoln

SESSION SEVEN BIBLE TUCK-IN™

A TRIBUTE TO MOM

EY VERSES

"A wife of noble character who can find? She is worth far more than rubies. Her children arise and call her blessed; her husband also, and he praises her." Proverbs 31:10,28

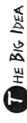IBLICAL BASIS

Proverbs 23:25; 31:10-31

THE BIG IDEA

Your mom is a gift from God. She is to be affirmed and honored.

WARM UP (5-10 MINUTES)

THE MOM SURVEY

- Divide students into groups with approximately six in each group.
- Give each student a copy of "The Mom Survey" on page 91 or display a copy using an overhead projector.
- Have students nominate their mothers for one of the following traits and tell why their mothers deserve the nominations.
- If time allows, have each group share who in their group has the most unique mom.

I nominate my mom as the one...
  With the most unique job.
  With the funniest laugh.
  Born in the smallest town.
  With the most unusual hobby.
  With the nicest smile.
  With the worst jokes (you must tell one of her jokes to the group and have them vote on the worst joke).

Does any mom have all these qualities? (Probably not; verse 10 indicates that it would be tough to find someone with all these qualities.)

- Instruct the students: "With your team members, discuss: Which verse, or verses, remind you of your mom? Why?" Give students a couple of minutes to discuss.

SO WHAT?

- Tell students: "Moms aren't perfect, but looking for the good in yours can improve your relationship with her. What can you do this week to show appreciation to your mom? Share with your team members what you will do. When everyone has shared, spend a few moments in prayer for one another to be able to show appreciation."

THINGS TO THINK ABOUT (OPTIONAL)

- Use the questions on page 95 after or as a part of "In the Word."

1. **The majority of teenagers say they feel closer to their moms than their dads. Why?**

2. How is a mother's nurturing love similar to the love of God?

3. What makes a mother's job difficult?

   In what ways is her job rewarding?

PARENT PAGE

- Distribute page to parents.

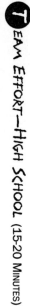

Team Effort—Junior High/Middle School (15-20 Minutes)

Mother Questionnaire

- Have students remain in groups of six.
- Give each student a copy of "Mother Questionnaire" on page 92 and a pen or pencil.
- Have the students discuss the first five questions in their small groups.
- Tell students to complete the last section individually.

Discuss the following questions with your group:

1. How would you describe your mom?
2. What is the best memory you have of your mom?
3. How are you like your mom?
4. On a scale of 1-10 (10 being the highest)
   a. How well does your mom listen to you?
   b. How well does she know you?
5. What is the most difficult conversation to have with your mom? Why?

Answer the following questions by yourself:

1. When was the last time you told your mom that you appreciate her? When was the last time you hugged her for no reason at all?
2. What are the pressures in her life?
3. What kinds of things cause her to become upset?

   Are your attitudes or actions sometimes the source of those things that upset her?

4. What are some changes she might be facing in her life that would cause her to be anxious?
5. Is your dad more of a help or a hindrance to her problems?

Team Effort—High School (15-20 Minutes)

Mom Reactions

- Have students remain in groups of six.
- Give each group a copy of "Mom Reactions" on page 93 or display a copy using an overhead projector.
- Have students discuss the following questions:

1. What would your mom do if...
   a. She caught you smoking a cigarette?
   b. She were elected Mom of the Year?
   c. You flunked math?
   d. You made your bed and took out the trash without being asked?
   e. You came home drunk?
   f. You wrecked the car?
   g. You were sick with a high fever?
2. How would you describe your mom to a friend who's never met her?
3. What's your favorite thing about your mom?
4. What's one thing your mom can't stand?
5. When you think of the word "mom," what's the first thing that pops into your head?

In The Word (25-30 Minutes)

Locate the Trait

- Divide the group into two to four teams.
- Read Proverbs 31:10-31 aloud.
- Make sure students have Bibles or copies of Proverbs 31:10-31. Tell them: "Since many moms are also wives, we'll use the verses I just read to discover some qualities of a good mother and wife. Stand up when you find a verse that supports or denies the statement I read. Each team will get a point when one of their team members is the first to answer correctly." (Provide a simple prize for the winning team members.)
- Option: A copy of "Locate the Trait" is available as a reproducible on page 94 for your optional use.

She has good business sense. (Supported by vv. 16,18)
She can make things and obtains the needed ingredients. (Supported by v. 13)
She is lazy. (Denied by vv. 17,27)
She doesn't care about poor people. (Denied by v. 20)
She is worth more than rubies. (Supported by v. 10)
She stays up late to complete projects. (Supported by v. 18)
She is not prepared for snow or other bad weather. (Denied by v. 21)
She laughs. (Supported by v. 25)
She sews, knits, crochets or does other needlework. (Supported by vv. 13,19)
Her husband doesn't trust her. (Denied by v. 11)
She is strong and dignified. (Supported by v. 25)
She worries. (Denied by v. 25)
She sleeps in and never makes breakfast. (Denied by v. 15)
Her children appreciate her. (Supported by v. 28)
Fearing the Lord is more important to her than charm and beauty. (Supported by v. 30)
She deserves a reward. (Supported by v. 31)

- Discuss the following with the whole group:

What she says makes sense and agrees with God. (Supported by v. 26)

SESSION SEVEN

A TRIBUTE TO MOM

Warm Up

The Mom Survey
I nominate my mom as the one...

With the most unique job.

With the funniest laugh.

Born in the smallest town.

With the most unusual hobby.

With the nicest smile.

With the worst jokes (you must tell one of her jokes to the group and have them vote on the worst joke).

SESSION SEVEN

A TRIBUTE TO MOM

Team Effort

Mother Questionnaire

Discuss the following questions with your group:

1. How would you describe your mom?

2. What is the best memory you have of your mom?

3. How are you like your mom?

4. On a scale of 1-10 (10 being the highest)
    a. How well does your mom listen to you?

    b. How well does she know you?

5. What is the most difficult conversation to have with your mom? Why?

Answer the following questions by yourself:

1. When was the last time you told your mom that you appreciate her? When was the last time you hugged her for no reason at all?

2. What are the pressures in her life?

SESSION SEVEN

 A TRIBUTE TO MOM

3. What kind of things cause her to become upset?

....
....
....

Are your attitudes and actions sometimes the source of those things that upset her?

....
....
....

4. What are some changes she might be facing in her life that would cause her to be anxious?

....
....
....

5. Is your dad more of a help or a hindrance to her problems?

....
....
....

SESSION SEVEN

A TRIBUTE TO MOM

Team Effort

Mom Reactions[1]

1. What would your mom do if...
   a. She caught you smoking a cigarette?

   b. She were elected Mom of the Year?

   c. You flunked math?

   d. You made your bed and took out the trash without being asked?

   e. You came home drunk?

   f. You wrecked the car?

   g. You were sick with a high fever?

2. How would you describe your mom to a friend who's never met her?

3. What's your favorite thing about your mom?

4. What's one thing your mom can't stand?

5. When you think of the word "mom," what's the first thing that pops into your head?

Note:
1. Adapted from Karen Dockrey and John Hall, *Holiday Specials and Boredom Busters* (Elgin, Ill.: David C. Cook, 1990), p. 43.

SESSION SEVEN

A TRIBUTE TO MOM

In the Word

Locate the Trait[1]

Read Proverbs 31:10-31. Make a check beside the following traits that are true to these verses in Proverbs.

- ❏ She is worth more than rubies.
- ❏ Her husband doesn't trust her.
- ❏ She has good business sense.
- ❏ She can make things and obtains the needed ingredients.
- ❏ She sleeps in and never makes breakfast.
- ❏ She is lazy.
- ❏ She doesn't care about poor people.
- ❏ She stays up late to complete projects.
- ❏ She is not prepared for snow or other bad weather.
- ❏ She laughs.
- ❏ She sews, knits, crochets or does other needlework.
- ❏ She is strong and dignified.
- ❏ She worries.
- ❏ Her children appreciate her.
- ❏ Serving the Lord is more important to her than charm and beauty.
- ❏ She deserves a reward.
- ❏ What she says makes sense and agrees with God.

Does any mom have all these qualities (see verse 10)?

....
....
....

Which verse or verses remind you of your mom? Why?

....
....
....

So What?

Moms aren't perfect, but looking for the good in yours can improve your relationship with her.

What can you do this week to show your appreciation for your mom?

....
....
....

Note:

1. Adapted from Karen Dockrey and John Hall, *Holiday Specials and Boredom Busters* (Elgin, Ill.: David C. Cook, 1990), p. 43.

SESSION SEVEN

A TRIBUTE TO MOM

Things to Think About

1. The majority of teenagers say they feel closer to their moms than their dads. Why?

   ....
   ....
   ....

2. How is a mother's nurturing love similar to the love of God?

   ....
   ....
   ....

3. What makes a mother's job so difficult?

   ....
   ....

   In what ways is her job rewarding?

   ....
   ....
   ....

SESSION SEVEN

A TRIBUTE TO MOM

Parent Page

Interview Your Mom
How did you feel when...

You married Dad?

....
....
....

I was born?

....
....
....

The last time you had to punish me when I did something wrong?

....
....
....

You had a fight with Dad?

....
....
....

You saw my last report card?

....
....
....

What gives you the most joy about our family?

....
....
....

SESSION SEVEN

A TRIBUTE TO MOM

QUESTIONS FOR THE STUDENT

What do you appreciate most about your mom?

What are ways you have seen your mom sacrifice for you?

If you could give your mom a "Most Valuable Mom" award, what would it say?

List, then tell your mom five reasons why you are thankful she's your mom.

1.

2.

3.

4.

5.

Session 7: "A Tribute to Mom"
Date

SESSION EIGHT

A FATHER'S LOVE

Key Verse

"But God demonstrates his own love for us in this: While we were still sinners, Christ died for us." Romans 5:8

Biblical Basis

Mark 10:13-16; 14:36; Romans 3:23; 5:8; 8:15,16; Hebrews 12:10

The Big Idea

A father's love comes in all shapes and sizes, but it's not always perfect. However, our heavenly Father is always approachable, and His love is both sacrificial *and* perfect.

Aims of This Session

During this session you will guide students to:

- Examine the similarities and differences between a father's love and the heavenly Father's love;
- Discover how they can better experience the heavenly Father's love and have a greater understanding of their earthly fathers' love;
- Implement a decision to develop a right understanding of their heavenly Father as well as develop a better relationship with their earthly fathers.

Warm Up

The Dad Survey—
A group activity to discover unique dads.

Team Effort— Junior High/ Middle School
Unconditional Love
A story from Jim Burns's childhood relating an earthly father's love to our heavenly Father's love.

Team Effort— High School
What Is a Dad?—
Students discuss things they like and don't like about their dads.

In the Word

A Father's Love—
A Bible study comparing a father's love with *the* Father's love.

Things to Think About (Optional)

Questions to get students thinking and talking about the important influence a father has on a person's concept of God.

Parent Page

A tool to get the session into the home and allow dads and young people to express their love for one another.

SESSION EIGHT

A FATHER'S LOVE

LEADER'S DEVOTIONAL

"Our fathers disciplined us for a little while as they thought best; but God disciplines us for our good, that we may share in his holiness" (Hebrews 12:10).

In early 1997, the tragic murder of Ennis Cosby, the 27-year-old graduate student and son of comic entertainer Bill Cosby, sparked an outpouring of compassion and nationwide grieving for perhaps America's most well-known father. Whether portraying Dr. Huxtable, Fat Albert or Moses, or laughing with children while pitching Jell-O, Bill Cosby's comedy routines, TV shows, recordings and books have caused millions of Americans to double over in the wonderful pain of side-splitting laughter. Now Bill Cosby's fans are watching their favorite father figure take a long, dark journey to the other side of laughter and joy. The death of his only son was never imagined when he wrote his nationwide best-seller *Fatherhood*.

It could be argued, I suppose, that more Americans identify with Bill Cosby as a father figure than they do with God. Perhaps it's because most of us have grown up with Bill Cosby teaching us to laugh with him about our common human foibles. Since television has become America's favorite babysitter, Bill Cosby has become a surrogate parent—the kind of dad many wished they had. Yet the reality of death and the zoom lens of TV news crews taking candid footage of a blank-faced, grief-stricken man in terrible pain has crumbled the image of a humorous, faultless, benevolent father. In his pain, we discovered that Bill Cosby is like all of us: broken, lost and in terrible need of a loving heavenly Father.

Perhaps the death of Ennis Cosby and the grief experienced by the whole Cosby family will bring us a little closer, a bit more in touch with the heart of God—the perfect Father who, two thousand years ago, allowed the brutal slaying of His Son to show us the depth of His love. Though we talk often about God's love and fatherhood, this is a reality we need to know, not just with our heads, but with our hearts. This lesson has the tools to help transform how your students understand, know and relate to God as their heavenly Father. It also has a message for youth workers: a reminder of God's sacrificial and unconditional love for *you*. The love of God, our heavenly Father, transcends joy and pain, laughter and grief. (Written by Joey O'Connor)

> **"No family should attempt an auto trip if the kids outnumber the car windows."**
> —Terresa Bloomingdale

SESSION EIGHT   BIBLE TUCK-IN™

A FATHER'S LOVE

 ### KEY VERSE

"But God demonstrates his own love for us in this: While we were still sinners, Christ died for us." Romans 5:8

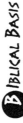 ### BIBLICAL BASIS

Mark 10:13-16; 14:36; Romans 3:23; 5:8; 8:15,16; Hebrews 12:10

 ### THE BIG IDEA

A father's love comes in all shapes and sizes, but it's not always perfect. However, our heavenly Father is always approachable, and His love is both sacrificial *and* perfect.

 ### WARM UP (5-10 MINUTES)

THE DAD SURVEY

- Divide students into groups with approximately six in each group.
- Give each student a copy of "The Dad Survey" on page 103, or display a copy using an overhead projector.
- Have students nominate their fathers for one of the following traits and tell why their fathers deserve their nominations.
- If time allows, have each group share who in their group has the most unique dad.

I nominate my dad as the one...
- With the longest hair.
- With the biggest feet.
- Who sings in the shower.
- With the least hair.
- Who was a star athlete in high school or college.
- Who tells the worst jokes. (You must tell one of his jokes and then have the group vote on the worst joke.)
- Who is the kindest. (Describe why and what he has done, then have the group vote on whose dad is the kindest.)

101

---

challenged, "Just Do It." The man was Jim Redmond, Derek's father.

"You don't have to do this," he told his weeping son.

"Yes, I do," Derek declared.

"Well, then," said Jim, "we're going to finish this together."

And they did. Jim wrapped Derek's arm around his shoulder and helped him hobble to the finish line. Fighting off security men, the son's head sometimes buried in his father's shoulder, they stayed in Derek's lane to the end.

The crowd clapped, then stood, then cheered, and then wept as the father and son finished the race.

What made the father do it? What made him leave the stands to meet his son on the track? Was it the strength of his child? No, it was the pain of his child. His son was hurt and fighting to complete the race. So the father came to help him finish.

God does the same for us. Our prayers may be awkward. Our attempts may be feeble. But since the power of prayer is in the One Who hears it and not in the one who says it, our prayers do make a difference.

How would you describe Jim Redmond as a dad?
What did he do to demonstrate his love for his son?
Describe a time when God comforted you in a time of need.
Describe a time when your father (or another person) comforted you.

SO WHAT?

What one concept from this Bible study helps you better understand a father's love?
How has this Bible study helped you understand your heavenly Father's love?

THINGS TO THINK ABOUT (OPTIONAL)

- Use the questions on page 110 after or as a part of "In the Word."
1. What makes our relationships with our dads so important to our concept of God?
2. Why is it difficult for someone who has a poor role-model for a father to have a healthy relationship with God as the heavenly Father?
3. Why is there no such thing as the perfect dad (see Romans 3:23)?
4. If someone does not have a good relationship with his or her earthly father, how can that person learn to understand and trust the perfect, loving, heavenly Father?

PARENT PAGE

- Distribute page to parents.

Team Effort—Junior High/Middle School

Unconditional Love

- Read the story "Unconditional Love" on pages 104-105.
- Have the whole group discuss the following questions:
  1. Is there a time in your life when you have had a similar experience with your dad (or another person important to you)?
  2. How was the love Jim's dad expressed in this story similar to the kind of love our heavenly Father offers to us?

Team Effort—High School (15-20 Minutes)

What Is a Dad?

- Give each student a copy of "What Is a Dad?" on page 106 and a pen or pencil.
- Give them five minutes to complete the page.
- Divide students into groups of three or four and have them discuss their answers with their small groups.

Newspaper columnist Charlie Shedd sponsored an "Appreciate Dad Contest." He asked people to write him and tell him the qualities of their dads they most appreciated. The following are the top ten most appreciated qualities of a great dad:

1. He takes time for me.
2. He listens to me.
3. He plays with me.
4. He invites me to go places.
5. He lets me help him.
6. He treats my mother well.
7. He lets me say what I think.
8. He's nice to my friends.
9. He only punishes me when I deserve it.
10. He isn't afraid to admit when he's wrong.

What are three qualities you appreciate in your dad? Circle any in the above list or write some new ones here:

Obviously, no dad is perfect. The following lists eight common gripes about dads:

1. He is too busy.
2. He isn't loving enough.
3. He doesn't listen.
4. He is too irritable.
5. He is often impatient.
6. He is too demanding.
7. He fights too much with Mom.
8. He watches too much TV.

What are three complaints you have about your dad? Circle any in the above list or write some new ones here:

This week in a constructive way share with your dad the three things you appreciate and the three gripes you have about him.

In The Word (25-30 Minutes)

A Father's Love

- Divide students into groups of three or four.
- Give each student a copy of "A Father's Love" on pages 107-109 and a pen or pencil, or display a copy using an overhead projector.
- Have students complete the study with their small groups.

A dad's love comes in all shapes and sizes. Some have a dad who could be the Father of the Year and others have an absent dad; either physically or emotionally. Perhaps your dad is your hero, a role model, your best friend or maybe he's your biggest burden. For some, Dad is gone—he died or left—but perhaps he is still present in your mind. No matter how your dad looks or behaves, he's very important to your spiritual life. The Bible calls God "our heavenly Father."

A Father's Love is Sacrificial. God's love is sacrificial.
Read Romans 5:8.
How did our heavenly Father *demonstrate* his love to you?

How has your earthly father (or another person important to you) demonstrated sacrificial love to you?

How has God demonstrated His sacrificial love?

A Father's Love is Approachable. God's love is approachable.
Read Mark 10:13-16.
How did Jesus make Himself approachable to the children?

Describe a time in your life when you felt this approachable kind of love from your own dad (or another person important to you).

Is He approachable to you today?

A Father's Love is Comforting. God's love is comforting.
Jesus revolutionized the concept of God when He referred to God as "My Father" and taught His disciples to address God as *Abba*, the Aramaic children's word for "father" or "daddy."

Before Jesus came, most Jewish people were taught not even to take the name of God upon their lips. They usually substituted terms such as "the most High," "from Heaven," "the Blessed," or "the Power" in place of His name. This made God seem impersonal and definitely not comforting. When they did refer directly to God or address Him, they called Him "God" or "Lord."

Jesus changed all this by referring to God as *Abba*. This made the concept of God approachable and comforting. For more examples of the use of the word "Abba" read Mark 14:36 and Romans 8:15,16. Now read the following example of a dad's love:

Jim Redmond is the kind of dad who is approachable and comforting. His son Derek, a twenty-six-year-old Briton, was favored to win the four-hundred-meter race in the 1992 Barcelona Olympics. Halfway into his semifinal heat, a fiery pain seared through his right leg. He crumpled to the track with a torn hamstring.

As the medical attendants were approaching, Redmond struggled to his feet. "It was animal instinct," he would later say. He set out hopping, pushing away the coaches in a crazed attempt to finish the race.

When he reached the stretch, a big man pushed through the crowd. He was wearing a T-shirt that read, "Have you hugged your child today?" and a hat that

SESSION EIGHT

A FATHER'S LOVE

Warm Up

THE DAD SURVEY
I nominate my dad as the one...

With the longest hair.

With the biggest feet.

Who sings in the shower.

With the least hair.

Who was a star athlete in high school or college.

Who tells the worst jokes. (You must tell one of his jokes and then have the group vote on the worst joke.)

Who is the kindest. (Describe why and what he has done, then have the group vote on whose dad is the kindest.)

SESSION EIGHT

A FATHER'S LOVE

UNCONDITIONAL LOVE

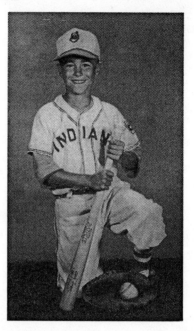

My boyhood goal was to play on the La Palma Little League All-Star team. It was now a reality. We were playing West Anaheim and I was pitching. What should have been a dream come true became a nightmare.

It started in the first inning: the lead-off hitter walked, the second guy hit a shot to right center field for a double, then I walked the third batter. With the bases loaded I hung a curve ball and the clean-up hitter cleaned up! He put that curve ball over the fence for a grand slam. Ouch!

I felt humiliated.

After only four batters the coach moved me to shortstop, where I made three errors in the next five innings! I also struck out twice. Needless to say, it wasn't a good day.

But now it was the last inning and I had a chance to redeem myself. We were tied up, 6-6, and the bases were loaded as I walked up to bat. Until this day, I had had the best batting average in the league. Despite my earlier strikeouts, everyone seemed confident that I could win the game for La Palma.

First pitch—I watched it go right over the plate: Strike one. Second pitch caught the corner: Strike two. I was feeling the tension. I stepped out of the batter's box and looked at my dad. He gave me the thumbs-up sign. The third pitch came straight down the middle of the plate. I watched it go by: Strike three!

I almost single-handedly lost the game! The other team emerged as the champions.

I had never been more miserable in my life. I cried like a baby. I didn't want to talk to

SESSION EIGHT

A FATHER'S LOVE

anyone, especially my dad. All my life he'd played catch with me, hit me grounders and threw batting practice. He'd been there to instruct and encourage me. Now, I'd let him down. I knew he'd be disappointed. I couldn't face him.

After unenthusiastically congratulating the other team, our coach told us it had been a great year. He said, "We should be proud." Yeah, right!

I couldn't put it off any longer. I had to face my dad. I slowly gathered my glove, bat and jacket, then looked up. There he was, running toward me. I knew I'd failed him. I was sure he was going to say something like "You should never watch three strikes go by when the bases are loaded."

Instead he rushed over to me, gave me a big bear hug and literally picked me up. Instead of anger there were tears in his eyes. And he said, "Jimmy, I'm so proud of you."

That night we ate a couple of cheeseburgers and drowned our sorrows in chocolate milk shakes. He told me a story about a time he'd failed miserably in the most important game of the season. We laughed and cried together. My dad never was very mushy, but when I saw the tears in his eyes, I knew he loved me and that everything would be okay.

Is there a time in your life when you have had a similar experience with your dad (or another person important to you)?

....
....
....

How was the love Jim's dad expressed similar to the kind of love our heavenly Father offers to us?

....
....
....

SESSION EIGHT

A FATHER'S LOVE

Team Effort

What Is a Dad?

Newspaper columnist Charlie Shedd sponsored an "Appreciate Dad Contest." He asked people to write him and tell him the qualities of their dads they most appreciated. The following are the top ten most appreciated qualities of a great dad:

1. He takes time for me.
2. He listens to me.
3. He plays with me.
4. He invites me to go places.
5. He lets me help him.
6. He treats my mother well.
7. He lets me say what I think.
8. He's nice to my friends.
9. He only punishes me when I deserve it.
10. He isn't afraid to admit when he's wrong.

What are three qualities you appreciate in your dad? Circle any in the above list or write some new ones here:

....
....
....

Obviously, no dad is perfect. The following lists eight common gripes about dads.

1. He is too busy.
2. He isn't loving enough.
3. He doesn't listen.
4. He is too irritable.
5. He is often impatient.
6. He is too demanding.
7. He fights too much with Mom.
8. He watches too much TV.

What are three complaints you have about your dad? Circle any in the above list or write some new ones here:

....
....
....

This week in a constructive way share with your dad the three things you appreciate and the three gripes you have about him.

© 1997 by Gospel Light. Permission to photocopy granted. *The Word on Family*

SESSION EIGHT

A FATHER'S LOVE

A Father's Love

A dad's love comes in all shapes and sizes. Some have a dad who could be the Father of the Year and others have an absent dad; either physically or emotionally. Perhaps your dad is your hero, a role model, your best friend or maybe he's your biggest burden. For some, Dad is gone—he died or left—but perhaps he is still present in your mind. No matter how your dad looks or behaves, he is very important to your spiritual life. The Bible calls God "our heavenly Father."

A father's love is sacrificial. God's love is sacrificial.
Read Romans 5:8.

How did our heavenly Father *demonstrate* his love to you?

....
....
....

How has God demonstrated His sacrificial love?

....
....
....

How has your earthly father (or another person important to you) demonstrated sacrificial love to you?

....
....
....

A father's love is approachable. God's love is approachable.
Read Mark 10:13-16.

How did Jesus make Himself approachable to the children?

....
....
....

Is He approachable to you today?

....
....
....

© 1997 by Gospel Light. Permission to photocopy granted. *The Word on Family*

SESSION EIGHT

A FATHER'S LOVE

Describe a time in your life when you felt this approachable kind of love from your own dad (or another person important to you).

....
....
....

A father's love is comforting. God's love is comforting.

Jesus revolutionized the concept of God when He referred to God as "My Father" and taught His disciples to address God as *Abba*, the Aramaic children's word for "father" or "daddy."

Before Jesus came, most Jewish people were taught not even to take the name of God upon their lips. They usually substituted terms such as "the most High," "from Heaven," "the Blessed," or "the Power" in place of His name. This made God seem impersonal and definitely not comforting. When they did refer directly to God or address Him, they called Him "God" or "Lord."

Jesus changed all this by referring to God as *Abba*. This made the concept of God approachable and comforting. For more examples of the use of the word "Abba" read Mark 14:36 and Romans 8:15,16. Now read the following example of a dad's love:

>   Jim Redmond is the kind of dad who is approachable and comforting.
>
>   His son Derek, a twenty-six-year-old Briton, was favored to win the four-hundred-meter race in the 1992 Barcelona Olympics. Halfway into his semifinal heat, a fiery pain seared through his right leg. He crumpled to the track with a torn hamstring.
>
>   As the medical attendants were approaching, Redmond struggled to his feet. "It was animal instinct," he would later say. He set out hopping, pushing away the coaches in a crazed attempt to finish the race.
>
>   When he reached the stretch, a big man pushed through the crowd. He was wearing a T-shirt that read, "Have you hugged your child today?" and a hat that challenged, "Just Do It." The man was Jim Redmond, Derek's father.
>
>   "You don't have to do this," he told his weeping son.
>
>   "Yes, I do," Derek declared.
>
>   "Well, then," said Jim, "we're going to finish this together."

© 1997 by Gospel Light. Permission to photocopy granted. *The Word on Family*

SESSION EIGHT

A FATHER'S LOVE

And they did. Jim wrapped Derek's arm around his shoulder and helped him hobble to the finish line. Fighting off security men, the son's head sometimes buried in his father's shoulder, they stayed in Derek's lane to the end.

The crowd clapped, then stood, then cheered, and then wept as the father and son finished the race.

What made the father do it? What made the him leave the stands to meet his son on the track? Was it the strength of his child? No, it was the pain of his child. His son was hurt and fighting to complete the race. So the father came to help him finish.

God does the same for us. Our prayers may be awkward. Our attempts may be feeble. But since the power of prayer is in the One Who hears it and not in the one who says it, our prayers do make a difference.

How would you describe Jim Redmond as a dad?

....
....
....

What did he do to demonstrate his love for his son?

....
....
....

Describe a time when God comforted you in a time of need.

....
....
....

Describe a time when your father (or another person) comforted you.

....
....
....

SO WHAT?
What one concept from this Bible study helps you better understand a father's love?

....
....
....
....
....

How has this Bible study helped you understand your heavenly Father's love?

....
....
....
....
....

© 1997 by Gospel Light. Permission to photocopy granted. *The Word on Family*

SESSION EIGHT

A FATHER'S LOVE

Things to Think About

1. What makes our relationships with our dads so important to our concept of God?

   ....
   ....

   Why is it difficult for someone who has a poor role-model for a father to have a healthy relationship with God as the heavenly Father?

   ....
   ....
   ....

2. Why is there no such thing as the perfect dad (see Romans 3:23)?

   ....
   ....
   ....

3. If someone does not have a good relationship with his or her earthly father, how can that person learn to understand and trust the perfect, loving, heavenly Father?

   ....
   ....
   ....

SESSION EIGHT

A FATHER'S LOVE

Dear Dad, I Love You[1]

The hospital seemed cold and abandoned as I walked down the quiet corridor. Fluorescent lights cast a haunting shadow over the lifeless furniture. Arteriosclerosis. What on earth does that mean?

My dad was scheduled the next day for quintuple bypass heart surgery. The conversation between my father and me amounted to small talk.

"What time is the surgery?"

"First thing in the A.M."

"Really?"

"Yep."

"Do you have everything you need? Can I get you anything?"

"No, I'm fine, Son, I'll be all right."

I stood in the dreary hospital room. I looked at my dad. The next words that came from my mouth were driven by something deep inside. "Dad, I love you."

As though launching from a high platform into a small pool of water hundreds of feet below, I had taken a blind leap of faith that seldom had been attempted in my family. I spoke three of life's most powerful, and too often most difficult words—I love you.

With the touch of a highly skilled surgeon, my father responded, "Son, I love you, too. I'll be okay. And I'll see you in the morning."

Thank God my dad was right.

Why is it so easy to say "I love you" to someone we've been dating, but so difficult to say those same words to family members? I've heard it firsthand. Kids do love their parents. Parents do love their kids. We just don't hear it said very often.

For Parents:

1. In what ways have you been shown love by your dad?

....
....
....

2. If you could say one thing to your dad, what would it be?

....
....
....

© 1997 by Gospel Light. Permission to photocopy granted. *The Word on Family*

SESSION EIGHT

A FATHER'S LOVE

3. If you could say one thing to your son or daughter, what would it be?
....
....

For Students:

1. In what ways have you been shown love by your dad?
....
....
....

2. If you could say one thing to your dad, what would it be?
....
....
....

3. What would you like to hear from your dad?
....
....
....

Note:
1. Doug Webster, *Dear Dad...If I Could Tell You Anything* (Nashville, Tenn.: Thomas Nelson Publisher, 1985), pp. 17-19.

Session 8: "A Father's Love"
Date ....

Unit III

STRESS

LEADER'S PEP TALK

You and I both know that many of the students who will go through this material with you have difficult home lives. When I first started in youth ministry, I think I was naive enough to actually believe that most of the kids in my youth group had stable home situations. Obviously, that is just not so. As we both know, kids in the church are not immune to problems in the home, and they desperately need tools to deal with some of the family problems they face on a daily basis. That's why this next section is so important.

Daryl was a guy in my youth group who came to the group because a friend invited him to one of our purely social events. As he now likes to tell it, "I came to meet girls!" Daryl's mom and dad had split up and although he hadn't shared the fact with his friends, he hated to go home because of all the tension he always felt as he came through the door. He actually had a much better time at the church youth event than he thought he would have and he even decided to visit the Bible study the next week.

To make a long and somewhat complicated story short, Daryl found in the youth group a family and eventually made a commitment to Christ, then felt God's tug to become a youth pastor. Today he is working with students primarily from broken homes and with his beautiful wife Karen is raising two great kids in a "transitional generation" home.

Scripture teaches us that we can inherit the "sins of a previous generation." The good news is that we can help many of our young people break the chain of dysfunction from a not-so-perfect-home situation and help them become the transitional generation who with the help of Christ will raise their children in more functional homes. And who knows, maybe there will be a Daryl or Karen in your group who will take your place helping the next generation of students build solid Christian families for the future.

> "Hear, O Israel: The LORD our God, the LORD is one. Love the LORD your God with all your heart and with all your soul and with all your strength. These commandments that I give you today are to be upon your hearts. Impress them on your children. Talk about them when you sit at home and when you

walk along the road, when you lie down and when you get up. Tie them as symbols on your hands and bind them on your foreheads. Write them on the doorframes of your houses and on your gates" (Deuteronomy 6:4-9).

SESSION NINE

RESOLVING CONFLICT

Key Verse

"Bear with each other and forgive whatever grievances you may have against one another. Forgive as the Lord forgave you." Colossians 3:13

Biblical Basis

Genesis 25:21-23,29-34; 27:1-45; 32:1—33:12;
Romans 12:18;
Colossians 3:13

The Big Idea

When biblical principles are properly applied to resolving conflict, family relationships become healthier and communication is clearer.

Aims of This Session

During this session you will guide students to:
- Examine the biblical principles of conflict resolution;
- Discover the many practical ways to resolve conflict;
- Implement effective biblical principles for conflict resolution.

Warm Up

The Great Diaper Race—
Students get a taste of parenting and have fun too!

Team Effort— Junior High/ Middle School

The Battle Cry—
Students rate the hot button issues in their homes.

Team Effort— High School

You Be the Counselor—
Case studies that ask for student advice.

In the Word

How to Resolve Conflict—
A Bible study examining the Genesis story of Jacob and Esau to learn practical guidelines for resolving conflict.

Things to Think About (Optional)

Questions to get students thinking and talking about practical ways to resolve conflict.

Parent Page

A tool to get the session into the home and allow parents and students to learn new ways to resolve family conflicts.

SESSION NINE

RESOLVING CONFLICT

Leader's Devotional

"If it is possible, as far as it depends on you, live at peace with everyone" (Romans 12:18).

Let's be honest. It's difficult to be in youth ministry very long without taking a personal inventory about the very issues we speak to teenagers about. In teaching young people about their spiritual lives, we are challenged to examine the depths of our own walk with God. By discussing sensitive topics, such as sexuality, we are forced to deal with our own sexuality. The same is true about drugs and alcohol, self-esteem, negative coping behaviors, thoughts, beliefs, attitudes, temptations and yes, even family conflict.

Effective youth ministry is not just about helping young people. It is also about what God is doing in your own life. As you know by now, the very same issues that touch teenagers in one way or another are some of the very issues with which youth workers are intimately acquainted as well. The young people in your youth ministry benefit from understanding how you have worked, or are working, through conflict in your own life. However, that doesn't mean you need to make personal pain or struggles a platform for seeking their input or support. In some cases, youth workers can develop an inappropriate dependency by sharing too much of their personal lives. Honestly communicating that God is still in the process of teaching you how to work through the conflicts you face each day is the best place to start.

How is this lesson on resolving family conflict related to your life? As you probably suspected, this chapter is as relevant to your personal life as it is to the young people in your group. Applying the spiritual principles of resolving conflict are important steps for all believers who want to honor God in all of their relationships. Are there any unresolved conflicts in your family that you've been putting off? Perhaps you've made previous attempts to be reconciled to someone in your family, yet the other person was unwilling to deal with the conflict. Whatever the condition of your family, we all know that no family is perfect. That's why taking a personal inventory of your family issues is an appropriate place to start in preparing to teach this chapter. A personal inventory will do you good. It may even do the kids in your youth ministry good. Honest. (Written by Joey O'Connor)

"Most people spend more time and energy going around problems than in trying to solve them."—Henry Ford

SESSION NINE   BIBLE TUCK-IN™

RESOLVING CONFLICT

Key Verse

"Bear with each other and forgive whatever grievances you may have against one another. Forgive as the Lord forgave you." Colossians 3:13

 Biblical Basis

Genesis 25:21-23,29-34; 27:1-45; 32:1—33:12; Romans 12:18; Colossians 3:13

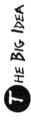 The Big Idea

When biblical principles are properly applied to resolving conflict, family relationships become healthier and communication is clearer.

Warm Up (5-10 Minutes)

The Great Diaper Race

- Divide students into four teams.
- Give each team a fully-clothed doll.
- Have each team select two people to take off their doll's clothes, put on a diaper and redress the doll. The fastest group wins. Using cloth diapers and pins will make this race even more exciting!

Things to Think About (Optional)

- Use the questions on page 122 after or as a part of "In the Word."
1. Why do so many families handle conflict poorly?

2. Who do you know that deals with conflict well? What do they do?

   What can you learn from them?

3. Describe an incident where Jesus handled conflict in a positive way.

 Parent Page

- Distribute page to parents.

Team Effort—Junior High/Middle School (15-20 Minutes)

The Battle Cry

- Give each student a copy of "The Battle Cry" on page 119 and a pen or pencil.
- Have each student rate his or her family's conflict points.
- When everyone has completed their ratings, display a copy of "The Battle Cry" using an overhead, or write the list on the board. As you read each item on the list, ask students to raise their hands if they chose that item as the number one cause of conflict in the family, then write the number of students who chose each item as the number one issue. Point out the one issue that got the most votes.
- Discuss the questions following the ratings chart.

Which of the following issues can turn your house into a war zone? Rank your top five conflict points, with number 1 being the worst.

___ A messy room
___ Coming home too late
___ Home responsibilities
___ Bad language
___ Phone use
___ Hairstyle
___ Sleeping habits
___ Eating habits
___ Choice of friends
___ Spending money
___ Church attendance
___ School performance
___ Clothing choices
___ Car use
___ Movie or TV program choices
___ Other _____

Why do you think our number one battle cry choice is _____?
Why do you think some of these issues are so important to parents?
Why do parents and teens have so many conflicts?

Team Effort—High School (15-20 Minutes)

You Be the Counselor

- Divide students into groups of three or four.
- Give each group a copy of "You Be the Counselor" on page 120.
- Have students discuss their advice in their small groups.

Read the following situations, then discuss the questions:

1. Kristen is a good kid most of the time. She and her mom are the best of friends and the worst of enemies, often in the same day. Kristen isn't always the best at obeying and her mom often nags her. One of their biggest problems is the phone. "That phone looks like it's connected to your head," is her mother's cry. Every night there seems to be a fight over the phone. "Kristen, have you done your homework?" "Kristen, you can't talk with anyone until you've washed the dishes!" "You have been on the phone for an hour." Use of the phone causes constant arguments and restrictions. Kristen talks back to her mother and then they blow up at each other.

They have come to you for counsel and advice. What advice would you give them?

2. Kristen's mom and stepdad have a hard and fast rule: You must tell the family where you will be at all times. Kristen agreed that was an okay rule. But on a regular basis she has broken the rule and disobeyed her parents. One day she walked to the nearby park with a friend without telling her parents. Another time she was across the street at the neighbor's, but her parents didn't know and they became frantic. Once she told her mom she was going to the library and instead went to an R-rated movie that she had already been told she could not see.

What advice would you give Kristen?
What advice would you give her parents?

In the Word (25-30 Minutes)

How to Resolve Conflict

- Give each student a copy of "How to Resolve Conflict" on page 121 and a pen or pencil, or display a copy using an overhead projector.
- Lead the students through the Bible study.
- As each principle and Scripture is read, comment briefly how each principle is applied in the story.

Jacob and Esau were in conflict even before their birth (see Genesis 25:21-23). That conflict continued into adulthood, and it wasn't correctly dealt with (see Genesis 25:29-34; 27:1-45). Eventually they did resolve their conflicts. There are at least six actions that helped them come to that resolution. These actions will work for you in whatever conflict situation you encounter.

Read their story in Genesis 32:1-20; 33:1-12, then read the following principles for resolving conflict and the accompanying verses beside each one.

1. Take the initiative in communicating the desire to resolve conflict (see Genesis 32:3-5).
2. Pray about the problem (see Genesis 32:9-12).
3. Identify the conflict or problem. Confess your fears (see Genesis 32:11).
4. See the other person's perspective and anticipate his or her possible resistance (see Genesis 32:13-20).
5. Tell how you feel (see Genesis 33:3,4).
6. Take action to correct the problem.
   - Make restitution if necessary (see Genesis 33:10,11).
   - Offer forgiveness and acceptance instead of seeking to get even or ahead (see Genesis 33:4,10,11).

The following verse is another important guideline:

> "Bear with each other and forgive whatever grievances you may have against one another. Forgive as the Lord forgave you" (Colossians 3:13).

So What?

Suggestions for improving conflict resolution:

1. Confess irresponsibilities.
2. Ask for forgiveness.
3. Write a letter. Carefully read it, then rewrite it before giving it.
4. Choose the time and setting wisely. Good communication occurs when everyone is rested and comfortable.
5. Play games that enhance self-expression. (Example: each family member shares worst day of my life, my most embarrassing moment, favorites, fears, positives seen in each other, what is fun, etc.)
6. Tell the person you want to solve the problem.
7. Seek help from a pastor, counselor or other professional.
8. Be patient and go slow.
9. Don't attempt to solve all your problems with one conversation.
10. Pray hard.

Who do you need to resolve a conflict with?
Which of these suggestions will be especially beneficial to your family?

SESSION NINE

RESOLVING CONFLICT

THE BATTLE CRY

Which of the following issues can turn your house into a war zone? Rank your top five conflict points, with number 1 being the worst.

___ A messy room
___ Coming home too late
___ Home responsibilities
___ Bad language
___ Phone use
___ Hairstyle
___ Sleeping habits
___ Eating habits
___ Choice of friends
___ Spending money
___ Church attendance
___ School performance
___ Clothing choices
___ Car use
___ Movie or TV program choices
___ Other _____

Why do you think our number one battle cry choice is _____?

....
....
....

Why do you think some of these issues are so important to parents?

....
....
....

Why do parents and teens have so many conflicts?

....
....
....

© 1997 by Gospel Light. Permission to photocopy granted. *The Word on Family*

SESSION NINE

RESOLVING CONFLICT

Team Effort

You Be the Counselor

Read the following situations, then discuss the questions:

1. Kristen is a good kid most of the time. She and her mom are the best of friends and the worst of enemies, often in the same day. Kristen isn't always the best at obeying and her mom often nags her.

One of their biggest problems is the phone. "That phone looks like it's connected to your head," is her mother's cry. Every night there seems to be a fight over the phone. "Kristen, have you done your homework?" "Kristen, you can't talk with anyone until you've washed the dishes!" "You have been on the phone for an hour."

Use of the phone causes constant arguments and restrictions. Kristen talks back to her mother and then they blow up at each other.

They have come to you for counsel and advice. What advice would you give them?

....
....
....

2. Kristen's mom and stepdad have a hard and fast rule: You must tell the family where you will be at all times. Kristen agreed that was an okay rule. But on a regular basis she has broken the rule and disobeyed her parents.

One day she walked to the nearby park with a friend without telling her parents. Another time she was across the street at the neighbor's, but her parents didn't know and they became frantic. Once she told her mom she was going to the library and instead went to an R-rated movie that she had already been told she could not see.

What advice would you give Kristen?

....
....
....

What advice would you give her parents?

....
....
....

© 1997 by Gospel Light. Permission to photocopy granted. *The Word on Family*

SESSION NINE

RESOLVING CONFLICT

IN THE WORD

HOW TO RESOLVE CONFLICT

Jacob and Esau were in conflict even before their birth (see Genesis 25:21-23). That conflict continued into adulthood, and it wasn't correctly dealt with (see Genesis 25:29-34; 27:1-45). Eventually they did resolve their conflicts. There are at least six actions that helped them come to that resolution. These actions will work for you in whatever conflict situation you encounter.

Read their story in Genesis 32:1-20; 33:1-12, then read the following principles for resolving conflict and the accompanying verses beside each one.

1. Take the initiative in communicating the desire to resolve conflict (see Genesis 32:3-5).
2. Pray about the problem (see Genesis 32:9-12).
3. Identify the conflict or problem. Confess your fears (see Genesis 32:11).
4. See the other person's perspective and anticipate their possible resistance (see Genesis 32:13-20).
5. Tell how you feel (see Genesis 33:3,4).
6. Take action to correct the problem.
   - Make restitution if necessary (see Genesis 33:10,11).
   - Offer forgiveness and acceptance instead of seeking to get even or ahead (see Genesis 33:4,10,11).

The following verse is another important guideline:

> "Bear with each other and forgive whatever grievances you may have against one another. Forgive as the Lord forgave you" (Colossians 3:13).

So What?

Suggestions for improving conflict resolution:

1. Confess irresponsibilities.
2. Ask for forgiveness.
3. Write a letter. Carefully read it, then rewrite it before giving it.
4. Choose the time and setting wisely. Good communication occurs when everyone is rested and comfortable.
5. Play games that enhance self-expression. (Example: each family member shares worst day of my life, my most embarrassing moment, favorites, fears, positives seen in each other, what is fun, etc.)
6. Tell the person you want to solve the problem.
7. Seek help from a pastor, counselor or other professional.
8. Be patient and go slow.
9. Don't attempt to solve all your problems with one conversation.
10. Pray hard.

Who do you need to resolve a conflict with?

Which of these suggestions will be especially beneficial to your family?

SESSION NINE

RESOLVING CONFLICT

Things to Think About

1. Why do so many families handle conflict poorly?

   ....
   ....
   ....

2. Who do you know that deals with conflict well? What do they do?

   ....
   ....
   ....

   What can you learn from them?

   ....
   ....
   ....

3. Describe an incident where Jesus handled conflict in a positive way.

   ....
   ....
   ....

SESSION NINE

RESOLVING CONFLICT

Parent Page

How Our Family Handles Conflict

Read Colossians 3:13.

How does this Scripture apply to family conflict?

....
....
....

Read through the following chart with your family:

Paths of Conflict[1]

THE PATH OF UNLOVING BEHAVIOR (Ego)

INTENT TO PROTECT Against Pain/Fear — Defensive/Closed — CONFLICT

AVOID PERSONAL RESPONSIBILITY for feelings, behavior and consequences —Be a Victim—

AUTHORITARIAN

- **CONTROL** Attempt to change child by disapproval, instilling guilt/fear

PERMISSIVE

- **COMPLIANCE** Give up self out of fear of conflict and disapproval
- **INDIFFERENCE** Withdraw emotionally and/or physically

NEGATIVE CONSEQUENCES FOR CHILD
- Low self-esteem
- Feels unloved
- Lack of personal responsibility
- Power struggles
- Tension/anxiety
- Angry/unhappy
- Develops protective behaviors

NEGATIVE CONSEQUENCES FOR CHILD
- Low self-esteem
- Feels unloved
- Lack of personal responsibility
- Uncaring/disrespectful
- Angry/unhappy
- Develops protective behaviors

NEGATIVE CONSEQUENCES FOR PARENT
- Self-esteem eroded
- Feels unloved, used, resentful toward child
- Feels tense, anxious, frustrated, unhappy
- Power struggles
- Parenting becomes a burden

THE PATH OF LOVING BEHAVIOR (Higher Self)

CONFLICT — Non-Defensive/Open — **INTENT TO LEARN**

ASSUME RESPONSIBILITY for feelings, behavior and consequences

LOVING INVOLVEMENT Caring for self and child

THE PROCESS OF EXPLORATION

CONDITIONS
- Open to being AFFECTED by child — Willing to experience transitory pain or fear from knowing the truth about self and child
- Open to knowing IMPORTANT REASONS for own and child's feelings/behaviors — Being nonjudgmental

AREAS
- What is the loving behavior in this conflict?
- **BELIEFS TO EXPLORE**
  - Fears
  - Protections
  - Consequences
  - Values
  - Expectations
  - Responsibility
  - Adequacy
  - Pain

POSITIVE CONSEQUENCES FOR CHILD
- High self-esteem
- Feels loved
- Cares about others
- Personally responsible
- Happy/peaceful
- Develops loving behaviors

POSITIVE CONSEQUENCES FOR PARENT
- Self-esteem enhanced
- Becomes a more loving person
- Feels secure, worthwhile
- Feels more joyful, peaceful
- Receives more caring from child
- Increased family intimacy

© 1997 by Gospel Light. Permission to photocopy granted. *The Word on Family*

SESSION NINE

RESOLVING CONFLICT

Discuss the following questions:

1. What is the typical way we handle conflict in our family?

   ....
   ....
   ....

2. Does each family member handle conflict in a different manner?

   ....
   ....
   ....

3. How can we improve the way we handle conflict?

   ....
   ....
   ....

Note:
1. Drs. Jordan and Margaret Paul, *Do I Have to Give Up Me to Be Loved by My Kids?* (New York: Berkley Books, 1995) p. 42.

Session 9: "Resolving Conflict"
Date ....

SESSION TEN

FRAZZLED FAMILIES

Key Verses

"One of [the Pharisees], an expert in the law, tested him with this question: 'Teacher, which is the greatest commandment in the Law?'

"Jesus replied: '"Love the Lord your God with all your heart and with all your soul and with all your mind." This is the first and greatest commandment. And the second is like it: "Love your neighbor as yourself." All the Law and the Prophets hang on these two commandments.'" Matthew 22:35-40

Biblical Basis

Isaiah 40:28-31;
Matthew 6:33; 22:34-40;
Philippians 2:4;
James 1:5

The Big Idea

Thriving families seek God first and set their priorities by His standards. Frazzled families are unfocused and too busy to develop strong relationships with one another and with God.

Aims of This Session

During this session you will guide students to:
- Examine the causes and effects of a frazzled family lifestyle;
- Discover the biblical principles of putting God's priorities first;
- Implement practical decisions to keep their family lives fruitful and free from unnecessary distractions.

Warm Up

How Do You Spend Your Time?—
An activity to make students aware of how their time is spent.

Team Effort—Junior High/Middle School

Overload—
Students take an inventory of their lives to identify areas of stress.

Team Effort—High School

The Balancing Act
Students complete charts that illustrate how balanced their lives are.

In the Word

First Things First—
A Bible study exploring the various aspects of the Great Commandment.

Things to Think About (optional)

Questions to get students thinking and talking about how to put God first.

Parent Page

A tool to get the session into the home and allow parents and students to discuss ways to deal with stress.

SESSION TEN

FRAZZLED FAMILIES

LEADER'S DEVOTIONAL

"Each of you should look not only to your own interests, but also to the interests of others" (Philippians 2:4).

For the first time in my life, I'm really beginning to see why teenagers live such busy and hurried lives—it begins at a very young age. As the father of three children ages 6, 2½, and 7 months, I am amazed at the number of activities that many parents involve their children in at younger and younger ages: swimming lessons, soccer teams, Indian Princesses, church programs, school plays, karate. It's no wonder that so many families feel chopped, sliced, diced and pureed at the end of the day. It used to be that everyone tried to keep up with the Joneses. Now everyone's trying to keep up with the Jones's kids.

If you have busy teenagers and frazzled families in your youth ministry, chances are the thorns of busyness didn't grow out of nowhere. Busyness is rooted in years of unfocused priorities and the irrational pursuit of activity. If the teens in your youth ministry seem bored or apathetic, think again: They may just be exhausted from the hectic schedule of their lives.

Teaching young people how to live balanced lives may be one of the greatest gifts you ever give them, and you must begin by living a balanced life yourself. You can model for young people how to establish priorities and when to say no. Though we don't like to admit it, our personal lives as youth workers often mirror the frazzled lives of the families we serve. We overcommit. We don't say no enough. As a youth worker friend of mine said to me, "We have too much 'bad busy' in our lives."

Our hearts can only dwell in peace when we learn to rest in Christ. Simplify. It's a critical principle for weeding out the thorns of busyness that choke our love for God. Maybe this lesson has come at the right time in your life. Listen to what the Spirit is saying to you about putting and keeping God first—yes, even before ministering to others. And hey, after you're done preparing this lesson, go take a nap! (Written by Joey O'Connor)

> "Peace is the deliberate adjustment of my life to the will of God."—Anonymous

SESSION TEN   BIBLE *TUCK-IN*™

FRAZZLED FAMILIES

*K*EY *V*ERSES

"One of [the Pharisees], an expert in the law, tested him with this question: 'Teacher, which is the greatest commandment in the Law?'

"Jesus replied: 'Love the Lord your God with all your heart and with all your soul and with all your mind.' This is the first and greatest commandment. And the second is like it: 'Love your neighbor as yourself.' All the Law and the Prophets hang on these two commandments.'"
Matthew 22:35-40

*B*IBLICAL *B*ASIS

Isaiah 40:28-31; Matthew 6:33; 22:34-40; Philippians 2:4; James 1:5

*T*HE *B*IG *I*DEA

Thriving families seek God first and set their priorities by His standards. Frazzled families are unfocused and too busy to develop strong relationships with one another and with God.

*W*ARM *U*P (5-10 MINUTES)

How Do You Spend Your Time?

- Give each student a copy of "How Do You Spend Your Time?" on page 129, or display a copy using an overhead projector.
- Assign a different student to read each statistic aloud after you have read each subtitle.
- Discuss the questions.

IN A LIFETIME, THE AVERAGE AMERICAN WILL:
- Spend six months sitting at traffic lights waiting for them to change.
- Spend one year searching through desk clutter looking for misplaced objects.
- Spend eight months opening junk mail.
- Spend two years trying to call people who aren't in or whose lines are busy.
- Spend five years waiting in lines.

---

3. How often do you and your family worship the King of kings and the Lord of lords at a church service?

Often   Sometimes   Never

How can putting God first in your life help in your family life?

How can putting God first help you with your priorities and time commitments?

LOVING YOUR NEIGHBOR MEANS BECOMING OTHERS-CENTERED

What do you think it means to love your neighbor as you love yourself?

Could your family members be considered your neighbors?

What happens if you are too busy to love your neighbors?

What specifically can you do to insure that you will develop a good relationship with your family?

LOVING YOURSELF

Think of someone you know who loves and takes care of him– or herself in a positive and healthy manner. What does this person do that demonstrates he or she has a balanced love of God, others and self?

What does it mean to you to love yourself?

How can you keep a healthy balance between loving God, others and self?

SO WHAT?

Using the illustration of car gears, here are different levels of our lives:

1. Park–A time for rest and renewal and recharging your batteries. Rest soothes, heals and gives perspective.
2. Low–Quality time for relationship building with family, friends and God.
3. Drive–Uses lots of energy, but it is a productive time. This gear is needed to perform your usual daily tasks.
4. Overdrive–Reserved for times needing lots of effort. You can't always stay in overdrive or you'll run out of gas sooner and eventually burn up the engine.

Which gear do you usually find yourself in?

Which gear is your family usually in?

Are there any decisions you need to make in order to put first things first in your life?

*T*HINGS TO *T*HINK *A*BOUT (OPTIONAL)

- Use the questions on page 136 after or as a part of "In the Word."
1. Sometimes life spins out of control. What do you do to get it back in perspective?
2. Why is it so easy to neglect our relationships with God and our families?
3. What advice would you give to someone who is struggling with putting God first in his or her life?

*P*ARENT *P*AGE

- Distribute page to parents.

- Spend three years in meetings.
- Learn how to operate 20,000 different things, from pop machines to can openers to digital radio controls.

IN ADDITION, THE AVERAGE PERSON WILL:

- Commute 45 minutes every day.
- Be interrupted 73 times every day. (The average manager is interrupted every eight minutes.)
- Receive 600 advertising messages every day (television, newspapers, magazines, radio, billboards).
- Travel 7,700 miles every year.
- Watch 1,700 hours of television every year.
- Open 600 pieces of mail every year.

Obviously most of these time crunches relate more to adults than students; however, which of these facts surprise you?

Name two areas of your life that take up the largest portion of your time.

 TEAM EFFORT—JUNIOR HIGH/MIDDLE SCHOOL (15-20 MINUTES)

OVERLOAD

- Divide students into groups of three or four.
- Give each student a copy of "Overload" on page 130 and a pen or pencil.
- Give students a minute to check off those factors that cause overload.
- Have students share their answers within their small groups and then help one another decide how to lessen their overloads.

Let's face it. Life sometimes gets too busy and our lives go into "overload syndrome." This means we take on more than we can handle.

TAKE THE OVERLOAD INVENTORY

Check three of the biggest overload factors in your life:

- ☐ Too many activities
- ☐ Making decisions
- ☐ Hurrying
- ☐ Noise
- ☐ Problems
- ☐ Schoolwork/work
- ☐ Commitments
- ☐ Parent pressures
- ☐ People
- ☐ Technology
- ☐ Competition
- ☐ Expectations
- ☐ Media
- ☐ Pollution
- ☐ Traffic
- ☐ Changes
- ☐ Money/debt
- ☐ Fatigue
- ☐ Church activities
- ☐ Other

List the three factors you've checked, and after each one, write what you can do to keep from going deeper into overload.

TEAM EFFORT—HIGH SCHOOL (15-20 MINUTES)

THE BALANCING ACT

- Give each student a copy of "The Balancing Act" on pages 131-132 and a pen or pencil.
- Display a copy of "The Balancing Act" charts using an overhead projector or draw the charts on a chalkboard, white board or poster board.
- Each graph represents both the degree of balance and importance of each aspect of a person's life. Point out the two sample charts of "A Typical Life" and "A Balanced Life." Discuss the sample charts with the students, then have them complete the blank charts entitled "The Real Me" and "The Balanced Life I'd Like to Have."
- Divide students into groups of three or four. Have them share their graphs and then discuss the questions at the bottom of the page.

 IN THE WORD (25-30 MINUTES)

FIRST THINGS FIRST

- Divide students into groups of three or four.
- Give each student a copy of "First Things First" on pages 133-135 and a pen or pencil, or display a copy using an overhead projector.
- Have students complete the study.

THE GREATEST COMMANDMENT

"Hearing that Jesus had silenced the Sadducees, the Pharisees got together. One of them, an expert in the law, tested him with this question: 'Teacher, which is the greatest commandment in the Law?' Jesus replied, '"Love the Lord your God with all your heart and with all your soul and with all your mind." This is the first and greatest commandment. And the second is like it: "Love your neighbor as yourself." All the Law and the Prophets hang on these two commandments'" (Matthew 22:34-40).

LOVING GOD MEANS PUTTING HIM FIRST

What does it mean to put God first in your life?

Rate yourself on the following scale:

1. How often do you spend a regular time alone with God?

Your Devotion to God

Often   Sometimes   Never

2. How often does your family spend time together in prayer?

Often   Sometimes   Never

SESSION TEN

FRAZZLED FAMILIES

How Do You Spend Your Time?

In a lifetime, the average American will:
- Spend six months sitting at traffic lights waiting for them to change.
- Spend one year searching through desk clutter looking for misplaced objects.
- Spend eight months opening junk mail.
- Spend two years trying to call people who aren't in or whose lines are busy.
- Spend five years waiting in lines.
- Spend three years in meetings.
- Learn how to operate 20,000 different things, from pop machines to can openers to digital radio controls.

In addition, the average person will:
- Commute 45 minutes every day.
- Be interrupted 73 times every day. (The average manager is interrupted every eight minutes.)
- Receive 600 advertising messages every day (television, newspapers, magazines, radio, bill boards).
- Travel 7,700 miles every year.
- Watch 1,700 hours of television every year.
- Open 600 pieces of mail every year.

Obviously most of these time crunches relate more to adults than students; however, which of these facts surprise you?

....
....
....

Name two areas of your life that take up the largest portion of your time.

....
....
....

SESSION TEN

FRAZZLED FAMILIES

OVERLOAD

Let's face it. Life sometimes gets too busy and our lives go into "overload syndrome." This means we take on more than we can handle.

Take the Overload Inventory

Check three of the biggest overload factors in your life:

- ❏ Too many activities
- ❏ Making decisions
- ❏ Hurrying
- ❏ Noise
- ❏ Problems
- ❏ Schoolwork/work
- ❏ Commitments
- ❏ Parent pressures
- ❏ People
- ❏ Technology
- ❏ Competition
- ❏ Expectations
- ❏ Media
- ❏ Pollution
- ❏ Traffic
- ❏ Changes
- ❏ Money/debt
- ❏ Fatigue
- ❏ Church activities
- ❏ Other _____

List the three factors you've checked and after each one write what you can do to keep from going deeper into overload.

1.

2.

3.

© 1997 by Gospel Light. Permission to photocopy granted. *The Word on Family*

SESSION TEN

FRAZZLED FAMILIES

THE BALANCING ACT

Most of us live a somewhat unbalanced life. The typical person has a difficult time balancing all the ingredients of a healthy life. Yet our goal is to try our best to live a more balanced life.

Study the following sample graphs to discover how a person might rate his or her life. The numbers along the side represent the degree of balance and importance each aspect rates in a person's life.

Sample Graphs

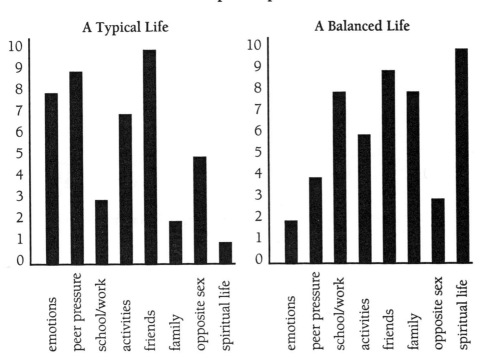

© 1997 by Gospel Light. Permission to photocopy granted. *The Word on Family*

SESSION TEN

FRAZZLED FAMILIES

Now take a few moments and rate your life as it is now and as you know it could be. Draw a line to represent the importance each aspect has in your life.

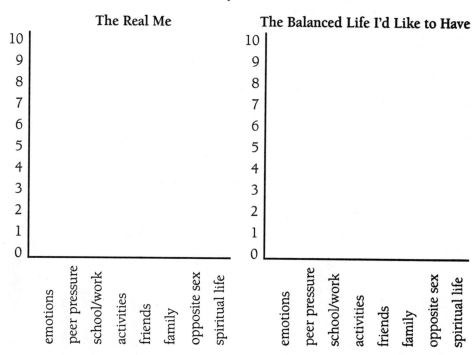

"And whatever you do, whether in word or in deed, do it all in the name of the Lord Jesus, giving thanks to God the Father through him" (Colossians 3:17).

1. According to Colossians 3:17, what should we do to develop balanced priorities in our lives?

   ....
   ....
   ....

2. What do you need to do to begin to live a more balanced life?

   ....
   ....
   ....

3. What step will you take this week toward that more balanced life?

   ....
   ....
   ....

Take a moment to pray for one another that you will take that important first step this week.

© 1997 by Gospel Light. Permission to photocopy granted. *The Word on Family*

SESSION TEN

FRAZZLED FAMILIES

FIRST THINGS FIRST

The Greatest Commandment

"Hearing that Jesus had silenced the Sadducees, the Pharisees got together. One of them, an expert in the law, tested him with this question: 'Teacher, which is the greatest commandment in the Law?'

"Jesus replied, '"Love the Lord your God with all your heart and with all your soul and with all your mind." This is the first and greatest commandment. And the second is like it: "Love your neighbor as yourself." All the Law and the Prophets hang on these two commandments'" (Matthew 22:34-40).

Loving God Means Putting Him First

What does it mean to put God first in your life?

....

....

....

Your Devotion to God

Rate yourself on the following scale:

1. How often do you spend a regular time alone with God?

| Often | Sometimes | Never |

2. How often does your family spend time together in prayer?

| Often | Sometimes | Never |

3. How often do you and your family worship the King of kings and the Lord of lords at a church service?

| Often | Sometimes | Never |

How can putting God first in your life help in your family life?

....

....

....

How can putting God first help you with your priorities and time commitments?

....

....

....

© 1997 by Gospel Light. Permission to photocopy granted. *The Word on Family*

SESSION TEN

FRAZZLED FAMILIES

Loving Your Neighbor Means Becoming Others-Centered

What do you think it means to love your neighbor as you love yourself?

Could your family members be considered your neighbors?

What happens if you are too busy to love your neighbors?

What specifically can you do to insure that you will be in a good relationship with your family?

Loving Yourself

Think of someone you know who loves and takes care of him- or herself in a positive and healthy manner. What does this person do that demonstrates he or she has a balanced love of God, others and self?

What does it mean to you to love yourself?

How can you keep a healthy balance between loving God, others and self?

SESSION TEN

FRAZZLED FAMILIES

So What?
Using the illustration of car gears, here are different levels of our lives:
1. Park—A time for rest and renewal and to recharge your batteries. Rest soothes, heals and gives perspective.
2. Low—Quality time for relationship building with family, friends and God.
3. Drive—Uses lots of energy, but it is a productive time. This gear is needed to perform your usual daily tasks.
4. Overdrive—Reserved for times needing lots of effort. You can't always stay in overdrive or you'll run out of gas sooner and eventually burn up the engine.

Which gear do you usually find yourself in?

....
....
....

Which gear is your family usually in?

....
....
....

Are there any decisions you need to make in order to put first things first in your life?

....
....
....

© 1997 by Gospel Light. Permission to photocopy granted. *The Word on Family*

SESSION TEN

Things to Think About

1. Sometimes life spins out of control. What do you do to get it back in perspective?

   ....
   ....
   ....

2. Why is it so easy to neglect our relationships with God and our families?

   ....
   ....
   ....

3. What advice would you give to someone who is struggling with putting God first in his or her life?

   ....
   ....
   ....

SESSION TEN

FRAZZLED FAMILIES

PARENT PAGE

SOLUTIONS FOR FAMILY STRESS

Have each family member rate what they believe to be the greatest cause of stress in your family by writing his or her initials by one of the following:

_____ Too many activities	_____ Work/School pressures
_____ Finances	_____ Anxiety/Worry
_____ Health problems	_____ Conflict
_____ Home responsibilities	_____ Other _____

Have family members share why they chose their particular cause.

Reducing Stress

Read Matthew 6:33 and James 1:5. How do these verses relate to the subject of reducing stress in your life?

....
....
....

Does your family have a regularly scheduled time for family devotions and prayer? If not, what prevents you from spending a specified time with God?

....
....

One important stress reducer is time to talk to one another. Sharing one another's thoughts and needs builds stronger relationships, and it lightens the load when others can share your burden and pray for you. Does your family have a regular daily time of connecting with one another in conversation such as at dinnertime or bedtime? If not, try to schedule a regular time right now.

Another great stress reducer is rest and relaxation. How often does your family plan a day, evening or weekend of fun? Take time right now to plan something for the very near future.

Do you regularly schedule time in each week for family fun and relaxation? If not, why not?

....
....
....

What activities or pressures could be lightened or dropped completely to simplify your family life?

....
....
....

© 1997 by Gospel Light. Permission to photocopy granted. *The Word on Family*

SESSION TEN

FRAZZLED FAMILIES

Dealing with Stress

There are times when stress is inevitable. In fact managed amounts of stress help us to accomplish important things. The secret is in relying on the Lord to help you manage stress properly. Here are two Scripture passages that help us deal with overwhelming pressures:

"I can do all things through Him who strengthens me" (Philippians 4:13, *NASB*)

"Do you not know? Have you not heard? The LORD is the everlasting God, the Creator of the ends of the earth. He will not grow tired or weary, and his understanding no one can fathom. He gives strength to the weary and increases the power of the weak. Even youths grow tired and weary, and young men stumble and fall; but those who hope in the LORD will renew their strength. They will soar on wings like eagles; they will run and not grow weary, they will walk and not be faint" (Isaiah 40:28-31).

Have family members share a pressure that seems to be overwhelming to them right now. Spend time in prayer for each family member and for wisdom in dealing with stress.

Session 10: "Frazzled Families"
Date ....

SESSION ELEVEN

DIVORCE

Key Verses

"'It has been said, "Anyone who divorces his wife must give her a certificate of divorce." But I tell you that anyone who divorces his wife, except for marital unfaithfulness, causes her to become an adulteress, and anyone who marries the divorced woman commits adultery.'" Matthew 5:31,32

Biblical Basis

Genesis 2:24;
Psalm 145:9;
Ecclesiastes 4:9-12;
Song of Songs 5:16;
Matthew 5:31,32; 19:3-9;
Romans 12:10,13,15;
Ephesians 5:21,25,28-31,33;
1 Corinthians 7:10-16;
James 1:27;
1 Peter 3:8; 4:8

The Big Idea

Divorce results in loss. Understanding the issues involved in divorce helps its victims find healing.

Aims of This Session

During this session you will guide students to:
- Examine the issues and circumstances of divorce and its effects on everyone involved;
- Discover what God's Word teaches on divorce;
- Implement a better understanding of the results of divorce and a strategy to love and welcome people of divorce with grace.

Warm Up

Famous Pairs—
Teams race to match pairs' names.

Team Effort— Junior High/ Middle School

Here's the Facts—
Students examine statistics on the effects of divorce on the family and society.

Team Effort— High School

Results and Reactions—
A discussion of how young people respond to divorce in their families.

In the Word

What Does the Bible Say?—
A Bible study that focuses on God's instructions about marriage and divorce, as well as how to treat the victims of divorce.

Things to Think About (Optional)

Questions to get students thinking and talking about the causes of divorce and how to apply this to their future marriages.

Parent Page

A tool to get the session into the home and allow parents and young people to focus on the problems of divorce and to pray for marriages of family and friends.

SESSION ELEVEN

DIVORCE

LEADER'S DEVOTIONAL

"The LORD is good to all; he has compassion on all he has made" (Psalm 145:9).

Erin was one of the most active, energetic students in our high school ministry. She went on all the winter and summer trips. She was on our Mexico mission leadership team. Active in sharing her faith with friends who weren't Christians, she regularly brought them to outreach events. Erin was the type of high school student that I wished I had ten more of.

All of Erin's energy and zest for life slowly began to change the day she found out about her father's affair which resulted in her parents' subsequent divorce. Erin's loss was as if someone had slit a tiny cut on her heart and slow internal bleeding had begun. Erin's love for God, her family and her friends slowly began to die.

Over the next two to three years, our youth staff witnessed Erin go through periodic emotional swings. Her attendance at youth events became irregular. She became overly dependent on the boys she dated. On the family front, Erin's mother was too busy pursuing a new degree and new boyfriends to pay attention to Erin's needs. Her mother spent weekends and at times even weeks away, leaving Erin and her sister at home alone. Sadly, when Erin graduated from high school, she jumped into the college party scene and abandoned her previously important commitments. Perhaps you know a few Erins?

You cannot be in youth ministry today without helping teenagers deal with the reality of divorce. Divorce devastates young people, but it doesn't have to destroy their faith. Share Erin's story with your youth group and ask what possibly could have been done to help her. For the students in your ministry who come from broken homes, your counsel, encouragement, role-modeling and comfort are what they may look to in the next few years to help fill the void of their fractured families. You can stand in the gap blown open by the devastation of divorce. (Written by Joey O'Connor)

"Jesus spoke more about trouble and crosses and persecution than he did about human happiness."
—W.T. Purkiser

SESSION ELEVEN   BIBLE TUCK-IN™

DIVORCE

KEY VERSES

"It has been said, 'Anyone who divorces his wife must give her a certificate of divorce.' But I tell you that anyone who divorces his wife, except for marital unfaithfulness, causes her to become an adulteress, and anyone who marries the divorced woman commits adultery.'" Matthew 5:31,32

BIBLICAL BASIS

Genesis 2:24; Psalm 145:9; Ecclesiastes 4:9-12; Song of Songs 5:16; Matthew 5:31,32; 19:3-9; Romans 12:10,13,15; Ephesians 5:21,25,28-31,33; 1 Corinthians 7:10-16; James 1:27; 1 Peter 3:8; 4:8

THE BIG IDEA

Divorce results in loss. Understanding the issues involved in divorce helps its victims find healing.

WARM UP (5-10 MINUTES)

FAMOUS PAIRS

- Prepare ahead of time index cards with the names of each of the following pairs (or some you come up with yourself). Write one name per card. Make identical sets of 10 to 15 pairs for each team into which you will divide the group. Be sure each set is well mixed.
- The following list is just suggestions from which to draw 10 to 15 pairs, but you can add some of your own—perhaps "famous" pairs in your group or church, the latest popular pairs in the media, etc.
- Optional: You can write the names (mixed up of course) on the board or an overhead transparency and give each team a piece of paper and a pen or pencil on which to write the matched pairs.
- Divide students into four approximately equal teams.

Make a list of what is lost in a divorce.

DIVORCE: THE CHURCH'S RESPONSE
Read Romans 12:10,13,15; James 1:27; 1 Peter 3:8; 4:8.
What does God's Word say about how we should relate to those who are troubled?

Read this case study and answer the questions that follow:

David's family looked like the perfect family. His dad and mom sang in the church choir. They were typical active members. David was a leader in the high school youth group and his sister was one of the most involved middle school students.
Then one day David's dad just left. He had been having an affair with a business associate for two years. David was devastated. He even told his youth pastor, "Perhaps it was my fault. I didn't talk to Dad enough about God. My sister and I argued too much."
David's sister was too embarrassed to show up at church because she thought everyone would talk about her. David's mom was trying her best to keep a good attitude in the midst of her pain.

1. What advice would you give the family?
2. As a friend of David, what could you do to help him and his family?

SO WHAT?
Brainstorm what the church can do to demonstrate love, welcome and acceptance to families of divorce.

THINGS TO THINK ABOUT (OPTIONAL)
- Use questions on page 148 after or as a part of "In the Word."
1. Why do you think there are so many divorces today?
2. In your opinion what is God's view of divorce?
3. What can you do to insure that your future marriage will survive?

PARENT PAGE
- Distribute page to parents.

SUGGESTED PAIRS:

Romeo & Juliet	Wally & The Beav
Hansel & Gretel	Ozzie & Harriet
Tom & Huck	Ricky & Lucy
Ren & Stimpy	Fred & Wilma
Garfield & Odie	Pebbles & BamBam
Pinky & The Brain	Cinderella & Prince Charming
Bill & Hillary	Adam & Eve
Jack & Jackie	Abraham & Sarah
Lyndon & Ladybird	David & Bathsheba
Ronald & Nancy	Ruth & Naomi
George & Martha	Mary & Joseph

TEAM EFFORT—JUNIOR HIGH/MIDDLE SCHOOL (15-20 MINUTES)

HERE'S THE FACTS

- Divide students into groups of three or four.
- Give each group a copy of "Here's the Facts" on page 143 and a pen or pencil, or display a copy using an overhead projector.
- Have each group read the facts and then discuss the questions.
- Have groups share their answers to question three with the whole class.

☐ There is one divorce every 27 seconds in the United States. That's over 1 million divorces a year.
☐ Ninety-two percent of children in a divorced home live with Mom.
☐ The average length of a second marriage is four to five years.
☐ Sixteen percent of 11- to 16-year-olds see their dads once a week after the divorce.
☐ Eighty-four percent of 11- to 16-year-olds see their dads less than once a week.
☐ Forty to fifty percent do not see Dad more than twice a year.
☐ Almost fifty percent of today's teenagers are affected in one way or another by divorce.
☐ Thirty-five percent of the families who get a divorce this year will move from a nonpoverty level of income to the poverty level next year.
☐ Three out of four teens who commit suicide come from families of divorce.
☐ Seventy percent of juveniles and young adults in correctional facilities did not grow up with both parents.

These facts hurt!
1. What is your reaction to these facts?
2. Make a check beside the fact that surprises you the most. Why does this surprise you?
3. What can people do to bring hope to people of divorce?

RESULTS AND REACTIONS

- Give each student a copy of "Results and Reactions" on pages 144-145, or display a copy using an overhead projector.
- Discuss the page with the whole group.
- Optional: Have an adult or student share about the pain they suffered during a divorce, ending with the positives that came out of his or her suffering.

Discuss the following:
1. What other results or reactions have you seen in families of divorce?
2. Which of these results or reactions make an impression on you?
3. What can someone do to survive the pain of divorce?
4. What can others do to help anyone who has experienced or is presently experiencing a divorce in the family?

IN THE WORD (25-30 MINUTES)

WHAT DOES THE BIBLE SAY?

- Give each student a copy of "What Does the Bible Say?" on pages 146-147 and a pen or pencil, or display a copy using an overhead projector.
- If you do not use an overhead projector, write the verses listed under "Marriage: God's Plan" on a chalkboard or poster board leaving space for the students' responses.
- Do the first section entitled "Marriage: God's Plan" with the whole group.
- Give each student a different Scripture reference to read and share with the whole group what his or her assigned verse says about marriage. If you have more students than verses, have them work in pairs. If you have more verses than students, have students read more than one verse.
- As the students share, write descriptive words or phrases next to each reference. The words and phrases in parenthesis are provided for your information.

MARRIAGE: GOD'S PLAN

Before beginning a study of divorce, we need to understand God's plan for marriage. Look up the following verses and write next to each reference a word or phrase that tells what marriage should be.

Genesis 2:24 (united, joined by God)
Ecclesiastes 4:9-12 (two together stronger than one, help one another)
Song of Songs 5:16 (lover and friend)
Ephesians 5:21 (submit/defer to one another)
Ephesians 5:25 (love as Christ loves)
Ephesians 5:28 (love as you love self)
Ephesians 5:29 (nourishes, cares for)
Ephesians 5:31 (be united, become one)
Ephesians 5:33 (love and respect)

- Divide students into groups of three or four.
- Have students complete the rest of the study in their small groups.

Divorce: Humanity's Way Out of God's Plan

Jesus has very strong words on the subject of divorce. Read and summarize the following:

Matthew 5:31,32
Matthew 19:3-9
1 Corinthians 7:10-16

Why do you think the New Testament is so strong when it comes to the issue of divorce?

SESSION ELEVEN

DIVORCE

Here's the Facts

- There is one divorce every 27 seconds in the United States. That's over 1 million divorces a year.
- Ninety-two percent of children in a divorced home live with Mom.
- The average length of a second marriage is four to five years.
- Sixteen percent of 11- to 16-year-olds see their dads once a week after the divorce.
- Eighty-four percent of 11- to 16-year-olds see their dads less than once a week.
- Forty to fifty percent do not see Dad more than twice a year.
- Almost fifty percent of today's teenagers are affected in one way or another by divorce.
- Thirty-five percent of the families who get a divorce this year will move from a nonpoverty level of income to the poverty level next year.
- Three out of four teens who commit suicide come from families of divorce.
- Seventy percent of juveniles and young adults in correctional facilities did not grow up with both parents.

These facts hurt!

1. What is your reaction to these facts?

2. Make a check beside the fact that surprises you the most. Why does this surprise you?

3. What can people do to bring hope to people of divorce?

SESSION ELEVEN

DIVORCE

Team Effort

Results and Reactions

It seems everyone involved in a divorce reacts differently. Here are eight common results of and reactions to divorce:

Results:

Pseudo-mature adolescent: They grow up quickly and typically don't have much time for teenage fun. They often get serious about a job to help the family.

Childish behavior: They get stuck at one age level and don't mature, but rather continue to display childish behavior. Some people in this category quit learning. They want to be taken care of.

Spouse replacement: Their goal in life is to make Mom or Dad happy. They try to meet most of the needs that a spouse would normally be able to meet.

Ping-Pong: They try to please both parents. They feel responsibility or pressure to keep everybody happy.

Money-wise: Finances are always on their minds. They often get consumed with money problems.

Misidentified: Perhaps they have lost the role model at home so they search for an identity outside the home. They may be easily steered by peer pressure or the pressure to identify with a social group.

Oversexed: Misses the warmth of the love of a parent so they seek attachment through a promiscuous physical relationship.

Jealous: They often sabotage Mom's or Dad's new relationships.

Reactions:

Loneliness: The sense of loss of relationship sometimes causes a great amount of loneliness.

Feelings of guilt: Many adolescents blame themselves for causing the divorce.

Inability to trust: They feel let down. It's hard to trust anyone, even God.

Withdrawal: Some deal with their pain by withdrawing. They get depressed and detach from church, activities, family and friends.

Anger: They express their feelings in destructive ways.

Misfit self-image: They feel like they don't fit in any longer.

SESSION ELEVEN

DIVORCE

Discuss the following:

1. What other results or reactions have you seen in families of divorce?

2. Which of these results or reactions make an impression on you?

3. What can someone do to survive the pain of divorce?

4. What can others do to help anyone who has experienced or is presently experiencing a divorce in the family?

SESSION ELEVEN

DIVORCE

What Does the Bible Say?

Marriage: God's Plan

Before beginning a study of divorce, we need to understand God's plan for marriage. Look up the following verses and write next to each reference a word or phrase that tells what marriage should be.

Genesis 2:24
Ecclesiastes 4:9-12
Song of Songs 5:16
Ephesians 5:21
Ephesians 5:25
Ephesians 5:28
Ephesians 5:29
Ephesians 5:31
Ephesians 5:33

Divorce: Humanity's Way Out of God's Plan

Jesus has very strong words on the subject of divorce. Read and summarize the following:

Matthew 5:31,32

Matthew 19:3-9

1 Corinthians 7:10-16

Why do you think the New Testament is so strong when it comes to the issue of divorce?

....
....
....

Make a list of what is lost in a divorce.

....
....
....

SESSION ELEVEN

DIVORCE

Divorce: The Church's Response

Read Romans 12:10,13,15; James 1:27; 1 Peter 3:8; 4:8.

What does God's Word say about how we should relate to those who are troubled?

....
....

Read this case study and answer the questions that follow:

> David's family looked like the perfect family. His dad and mom sang in the church choir. They were typical active members. David was a leader in the high school youth group and his sister was one of the most involved middle school students.
>
> Then one day David's dad just left. He had been having an affair with a business associate for two years. David was devastated. He even told his youth pastor, "Perhaps it was my fault. I didn't talk to Dad enough about God. My sister and I argued too much."
>
> David's sister was too embarrassed to show up at church because she thought everyone would talk about her. David's mom was trying her best to keep a good attitude in the midst of her pain.

1. What advice would you give the family?

....
....
....

2. As a friend of David, what could you do to help him and his family?

....
....
....

SO WHAT?
Brainstorm what the Church can do to demonstrate love, welcome and acceptance to families of divorce.

SESSION ELEVEN

DIVORCE

Things to Think About

1. Why do you think there are so many divorces today?

   ....
   ....
   ....

2. In your opinion what is God's view of divorce?

   ....
   ....
   ....

3. What can you do to insure that your future marriage will survive?

   ....
   ....
   ....

SESSION ELEVEN

DIVORCE

DIVORCE AND THE FAMILY

- Half of America's young people will live in a home where there is a divorce.
- Seventy-five percent of juveniles and young adults in correctional facilities did not grow up with both parents.
- Three out of four teenagers who commit suicide come from families of divorce.
- Forty to fifty percent of teenagers ages 11 to 16 see their dads less than three times a year.

God's Intention for Marriage

Read the following Scripture references concerning God's plan for marriage. Then as a family discuss the following questions which apply to your family situation.

    Genesis 2:24   Ecclesiastes 4:9-12
    Song of Songs 5:16   Ephesians 5:21-33

For parents who are not divorced:

1. What is it like for your teenager when you and your spouse disagree?

2. What are you doing—both good and bad—to model how to deal with conflict and differences?

3. What areas of your relationship do you need to bring more into alignment with God's intention for marriage?

For students whose parents are not divorced:
1. How do you feel when your parents disagree?

2. How have your parents modeled a godly marriage to you?

SESSION ELEVEN

DIVORCE

3. What concerns you about your parents' relationship?
   ....
   ....

For divorced or separated families:
1. How have your children been affected by your separation/divorce?
   ....
   ....

2. Discuss the effects of your separation/divorce with your teen. Ask him or her the following:
   a. What is causing you pain right now?
   b. What can I do to help you deal with your pain?
   c. What have you lost as a result of the separation/divorce?

3. List the top three issues that arise during the holidays.
   ....
   ....
   ....

For students whose parents are separated or divorced:
1. What issues are bothering you about your parents' separation?
   ....
   ....
   ....

2. How can your parents help you deal with your struggles or pain?
   ....
   ....
   ....

3. Who/what has been helpful to you during this difficult time?
   ....
   ....
   ....

Take a few moments to pray for marriages in your family and extended family.

Session 11: "Divorce"
Date ....

SESSION TWELVE

FAMILY CRISES

Key Verses

"The LORD is my shepherd, I shall not be in want. He makes me lie down in green pastures, he leads me beside quiet waters, he restores my soul. He guides me in paths of righteousness for his name's sake. Even though I walk through the valley of the shadow of death, I will fear no evil, for you are with me; your rod and your staff they comfort me. You prepare a table before me in the presence of my enemies. You anoint my head with oil; my cup overflows. Surely goodness and love will follow me all the days of my life, and I will dwell in the house of the LORD forever." Psalm 23

Biblical Basis

Exodus 17:8-13;
Deuteronomy 31:8;
Nehemiah 8:10;
Psalm 23; 103:17; 130:3,4;
Proverbs 15:22;
Ecclesiastes 4:9,10,12;
Isaiah 54:10; 66:13;
Matthew 11:28-30; 28:20;
John 3:16; 11:32-44; 14:26; 16:13,24,33;
Acts 10:43;
Ephesians 3:12;
1 John 1:9

The Big Idea

Every family experiences crises at one time or another. There are biblical answers to help anyone working through these difficult times.

Aims of This Session

During this session you will guide students to:
- Examine the pain and difficulties related to family hardships and problems;
- Discover how to deal with these painful experiences and find hope;
- Implement a biblical plan to give or receive help and hope for others when they experience suffering.

Warm Up

Family Feud—
A role play of how a parent or student responds to a difficult situation.

Team Effort— Junior High/ Middle School

Footprints—
Students relate Psalm 23 to this famous poem.

Team Effort— High School

The Causes of Crises—
Students list and discuss experiences that cause problems in any family.

In the Word

Hope, Help and Healing—
A Bible study focusing on the hope, help and healing that God provides those who are suffering.

Things to Think About (optional)
Questions to get students thinking and talking about how to deal with their own or others' suffering.

Parent Page
A tool to get the session into the home and allow parents and young people to discover the biblical way to deal with suffering.

SESSION TWELVE

FAMILY CRISES

LEADER'S DEVOTIONAL

"As a mother comforts her child, so will I comfort you" (Isaiah 66:13).

I just finished reading the life story of baseball legend Mickey Mantle. This American tale of alcoholism, adultery and the subsequent trauma experienced by his family is a sobering testimony from one of America's greatest heroes. Ironically, on his deathbed Mickey Mantle said, "If you want an example of how to live your life, don't look at me. I'm no hero."

When Mantle's alcohol abuse was followed by the alcoholism of his wife and four sons, he courageously entered drug recovery treatment and as a result he reconciled his broken relationships with his wife and sons. Turning tragedy into triumph, Mickey Mantle also prayed to receive Christ with ex-baseball-great-turned-minister Bobby Richardson. Before his death by cancer and a failed kidney transplant, Mantle received thousands of letters from fans who entered alcohol treatment because of his example. In their letters fans wrote, "I figured if you could admit to being an alcoholic and enter treatment then so could I." Now that's what I call a home run.

By raising the subject of crisis in the home with this Bible study, you are bound to be busy meeting with a number of students in the next few weeks. It's impossible to talk about alcoholism, drug abuse, violence, divorce or sexual abuse without having a student tap you on the shoulder and say, "Can we talk?"

Just as Mickey Mantle was a key in motivating others to enter recovery, you are an essential part of helping kids in crises. You can offer the help, hope, compassion and comfort of Christ teenagers are seeking in response to their pain. This chapter will provide you with helpful ideas, biblical principles and proven strategies for helping teenagers deal with difficult times in their homes. As you make yourself available to the Holy Spirit, simply ask for wisdom in dealing with each individual problem. God promises you the wisdom, knowledge and guidance you need to help young people in the healing process. If you encounter a situation beyond your experience or capability to handle, never be afraid to ask for help. You're not called to hit a home run with a crisis you can't handle. Your wisest move may be calling in a pinch hitter. (Written by Joey O'Connor)

> "It always looks darkest just before it gets totally black."
> —Charlie Brown

SESSION TWELVE   BIBLE TUCK-IN™

FAMILY CRISES

KEY VERSES

"The LORD is my shepherd, I shall not be in want. He makes me lie down in green pastures, he leads me beside quiet waters, he restores my soul. He guides me in paths of righteousness for his name's sake. Even though I walk through the valley of the shadow of death, I will fear no evil, for you are with me; your rod and your staff they comfort me. You prepare a table before me in the presence of my enemies. You anoint my head with oil; my cup overflows. Surely goodness and love will follow me all the days of my life, and I will dwell in the house of the LORD forever." Psalm 23

BIBLICAL BASIS

Exodus 17:8-13; Deuteronomy 31:8; Nehemiah 8:10; Psalm 23; 103:17; 130:3,4; Proverbs 15:22; Ecclesiastes 4:9,10,12; Isaiah 54:10; 66:13; Matthew 11:28-30; 28:20; John 3:16; 11:32-44; 14:26; 16:13,24,33; Acts 10:43; Ephesians 3:12; 1 John 1:9

THE BIG IDEA

Every family experiences crises at one time or another. There are biblical answers to help anyone working through these difficult times.

WARM UP (5-10 MINUTES)

FAMILY FEUD
- Choose two individuals from your group to role-play a family disagreement.
- Person A explains to the group one of his or her latest problems, fights or disagreements with his or her family. Person B role-plays the parent, responding by sharing his/her feelings from the point of view of the parent.
- After a brief time of interaction, have the group discuss the problem from both angles and try to come up with a workable solution for all.
- This can be done as many times as you wish by having new people role-play a situation.

153

"'In me you may have peace. In this world you will have trouble. But take heart! I have overcome the world'" (John 16:33).

How do these words of Jesus give you hope?

4. God cares. He really does!
Frankly, most people who have experienced any kind of crisis in their home often struggle with their relationship with God. Too many people spend much of their energy blaming God instead of being comforted by Him.
God wants to walk with you through your valley of hurt and disappointment. All you need to do is reach out and take His hand. God weeps with you in your tragedy. He loves you and wants to heal your wounds.
Read Psalm 23. What comfort does this psalm offer?

SO WHAT?
Read John 11:32-44. What does this passage tell you about Jesus?

Jesus knew that he would raise Lazarus from the dead, but He wept. Why? (v. 33)

What does this tell you about the character of God?

One of the great truths is that we have a God who sheds tears when someone is in pain. The fact that Christ wept at the death of a friend should encourage you that He surely cares for those with pain in their lives.
Give Him your pain and your sorrows. He has promised, "'Come to me, all you who are weary and burdened, and I will give you rest. Take my yoke upon you and learn from me, for I am gentle and humble in heart, and you will find rest for your souls. For my yoke is easy and my burden is light'" (Matthew 11:28-30).

THINGS TO THINK ABOUT (OPTIONAL)

- Use questions on page 159 after or as a part of "In the Word."
1. How can you help a friend who is experiencing a family hardship?

2. What traumatic situations require the help of a professional counselor?

3. What do you think the statement "before freedom comes pain" means?

PARENT PAGE
- Distribute page to parents.

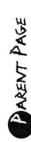

Team Effort—Junior High/Middle School (15-20 Minutes)

Footprints

- Give each student a copy of "Footprints" on page 155, or display a copy using an overhead projector.
- Have students read the story, then discuss the questions.
- Option: You could read the story aloud and discuss the questions with the students.

What is the good news from this story?

How can you apply it to your own life?

Read Psalm 23. How can the image of Jesus as the loving Shepherd comfort you when you are having a difficult time? Have you experienced a time when you have felt God's loving presence or comfort? Please describe it for us.

Team Effort—High School (15-20 Minutes)

The Causes of Crises

- Divide students into groups of five or six and give each group a piece of paper and a pen or pencil.
- Give the small groups two to three minutes to list as many different things they can think of that cause suffering for families. The following is a list of possible responses:

Divorce	Death
Illness	Physical, sexual, or emotional abuse
Sexual promiscuity	Adultery
Absence of Dad/Mom	Substance abuse
Workaholic	Suicide
Occultism	Homosexuality
AIDS	Addictions to pornography, gambling, etc.
Runaways	Eating disorders
Murder/violence	Loss of job, poverty

- Ask the group with the longest list to read their responses. Ask the other groups to add any different items not mentioned.
- Discuss the following question:

How many of you have experienced at least one of the difficulties we have listed? (Point out that every family experiences difficult times in varying degrees.)

In The Word (25-30 Minutes)

Hope, Help and Healing

- Divide students into groups of three or four.
- Give each student a copy of "Hope, Help and Healing" on pages 156-158 and a pen or pencil, or display a copy using an overhead projector.
- Have students complete the study in their small groups.

The odds are great that either you or a close friend of yours has experienced family hardship. Home is not always a happy place. Millions of people suffer in silence. Scripture is clear that even in the most difficult situations there is hope, help and healing from God.

Possible Solutions for Negative Situations

1. Realize and accept the fact that the crisis is not necessarily your fault. Far too many people blame themselves for their difficult situation. Sometimes our troubles are caused by our sin or the sins of others. If it is caused by our own sin, we need to deal with that through prayer and confession (see 1 John 1:9). If you are suffering because of the sin of others, you will need to ask God to help you deal with the consequences of the sins of others. There are yet other times when the crisis may not be the direct result of sin, but simply due to the circumstances of being human in an imperfect world, such as a serious illness or an accident. God has promised us that He will help us through the difficult times.

- Tom blamed himself for his parents' divorce.
- Sherri felt she must have been subconsciously flirting with the person who abused her.
- When Jerry's uncle committed suicide, he thought, *I should have talked to my uncle about God.*

How do each one of these situations demonstrate wrong thinking when it comes to laying the blame?

What areas of your life do you tend to blame yourself for when in actuality it's not all your fault?

2. Seek help. Don't suffer in silence.

"Plans fail for lack of counsel, but with many advisers they succeed" (Proverbs 15:22). "Two are better than one...If one falls down, his friend can help him up....A cord of three strands is not quickly broken" (Ecclesiastes 4:9,10,12).

What do these verses say about seeking help?

Why do people with traumatic home situations not talk with anyone or ask for help?

Why is it so important and healthy to seek help rather than suffer in silence?

3. There is hope.

Many people come out of traumatic home situations battered and bruised, but they get through the process and live very productive lives.

"The LORD himself goes before you and will be with you; he will never leave you nor forsake you. Do not be afraid; do not be discouraged" (Deuteronomy 31:8).

What is the hope found in this verse?

SESSION TWELVE

FAMILY CRISES

FOOTPRINTS

One night a man had a dream. He dreamed he was walking along the beach with the Lord. Across the sky flashed scenes from his life. For each scene, he noticed two sets of footprints in the sand; one belonging to him and the other to the Lord.

When the last scene of his life flashed before him, he looked back at the footprints in the sand. He noticed that many times along the path of his life there was only one set of footprints. He also noticed that it happened at the very lowest and saddest times in his life.

This really bothered him and he questioned the Lord about it: "Lord, you said that once I decided to follow You, You'd walk with me all the way. But I have noticed that during the most troublesome times in my life, there is only one set of footprints. I don't understand why when I needed You most, You would leave me."

The Lord replied, "My precious, precious child. I love you and would never leave you. During your times of trial and suffering, when you see only one set of footprints, it was then that I carried you."—Author unknown

What is the good news from this story?

....
....
....

How can you apply it to your own life?

....
....
....

Read Psalm 23. How can the image of Jesus as the loving Shepherd comfort you when you are having a difficult time?

....
....
....

Have you experienced a time when you have felt God's loving presence or comfort? Please describe it for us.

....
....
....

© 1997 by Gospel Light. Permission to photocopy granted. *The Word on Family*

SESSION TWELVE

FAMILY CRISES

In the Word

Hope, Help and Healing

The odds are great that either you or a close friend of yours has experienced family hardship. Home is not always a happy place. Millions of people suffer in silence. Scripture is clear that even in the most difficult situations there is hope, help and healing from God.

Possible solutions for negative situations

1. Realize and accept the fact that the crisis is not necessarily your fault.

Far too many people blame themselves for their difficult situation. Sometimes our troubles are caused by our sin or the sins of others. If it is caused by our own sin, we need to deal with that through prayer and confession (see 1 John 1:9). If you are suffering because of the sin of others, you will need to ask God to help you deal with the consequences of the sins of others.

There are yet other times when the crisis may not be the direct result of sin, but simply due to the circumstances of being human in an imperfect world, such as a serious illness or an accident. God has promised us that He will help us through the difficult times.

What areas of your life do you tend to blame yourself for when in actuality it's not all your fault?

....
....
....

- Tom blamed himself for his parents' divorce.
- Sherri felt she must have been subconsciously flirting with the person who abused her.
- When Jerry's uncle committed suicide, he thought, *I should have talked to my uncle about God.*

How do each one of these situations demonstrate wrong thinking when it comes to laying the blame?

....
....
....

2. Seek help. Don't suffer in silence.

"Plans fail for lack of counsel, but with many advisers they succeed" (Proverbs 15:22).

"Two are better than one…If one falls down, his friend can help him up…. A cord of three strands is not quickly broken" (Ecclesiastes 4:9,10,12).

SESSION TWELVE

FAMILY CRISES

What do these verses say about seeking help?

Why do people with traumatic home situations not talk with anyone or ask for help?

Why is it so important and healthy to seek help rather than suffer in silence?

3. **There is hope.**
   Many people come out of traumatic home situations battered and bruised, but they get through the process and live very productive lives.

   > "The Lord himself goes before you and will be with you; he will never leave you nor forsake you. Do not be afraid; do not be discouraged" (Deuteronomy 31:8).

   What is the hope found in this verse?

   > "'In me you may have peace. In this world you will have trouble. But take heart! I have overcome the world'" (John 16:33).

   How do these words of Jesus give you hope?

4. **God cares. He really does!**
   Frankly, most people who have experienced any kind of crisis in their home often struggle with their relationship with God. Too many people spend much of their energy blaming God instead of being comforted by Him.

© 1997 by Gospel Light. Permission to photocopy granted. *The Word on Family*

SESSION TWELVE

FAMILY CRISES

God wants to walk with you through your valley of hurt and disappointment. All you need to do is reach out and take His hand. God weeps with you in your tragedy. He loves you and wants to heal your wounds.

Read Psalm 23. What comfort does this psalm offer?

....
....
....

So What?

Read John 11:32-44. What does this passage tell you about Jesus?

....
....
....

Jesus knew that he would raise Lazarus from the dead, but He wept. Why? (v. 33)

....
....
....

What does this tell you about the character of God?

....
....
....

One of the great truths is that we have a God who sheds tears when someone is in pain. The fact that Christ wept at the death of a friend should encourage you that He surely cares for those with pain in their lives.

Give Him your pain and your sorrows. He has promised, "'Come to me, all you who are weary and burdened, and I will give you rest. Take my yoke upon you and learn from me, for I am gentle and humble in heart, and you will find rest for your souls. For my yoke is easy and my burden is light'" (Matthew 11:28-30).

SESSION TWELVE

FAMILY CRISES

Things to Think About

1. How can you help a friend who is experiencing a family hardship?

   ....
   ....
   ....

2. What traumatic situations require the help of a professional counselor?

   ....
   ....
   ....

3. What do you think the statement "before freedom comes pain" means?

   ....
   ....
   ....

SESSION TWELVE

FAMILY CRISES

Parent Page

COMFORT TO THOSE WHO ARE SUFFERING

The Bible contains over 3,000 promises made by God. The following are some of the promises that may be very comforting for those experiencing a crisis in the home.

Read the following Scriptures together and have each family member select one passage that is particularly meaningful and tell why.

Theme	Promise
Love	"'Though the mountains be shaken and the hills be removed, yet my unfailing love for you will not be shaken nor my covenant of peace be removed,' says the LORD, who has compassion on you" (Isaiah 54:10).
	"'For God so loved the world that he gave his one and only Son, that whoever believes in him shall not perish but have eternal life'" (John 3:16).
Forgiveness	"If we confess our sins, he is faithful and just and will forgive us our sins and purify us from all unrighteousness" (1 John 1:9).
	"All the prophets testify about him that everyone who believes in him receives forgiveness of sins through his name" (Acts 10:43).
Comfort	"But from everlasting to everlasting the LORD's love is with those who fear him, and his righteousness with their children's children" (Psalm 103:17).
	"'And surely I am with you always, to the very end of the age'" (Matthew 28:20).
Guidance	"'But the Counselor, the Holy Spirit, whom the Father will send in my name, will teach you all things and will remind you of everything I have said to you'" (John 14:26).
	"'But when he, the Spirit of truth, comes, he will guide you into all truth. He will not speak on his own; he will speak only what he hears, and he will tell you what is yet to come'" (John 16:13).
Joy	"Nehemiah said, 'Go and enjoy choice food and sweet drinks, and send some to those who have nothing prepared. This day is sacred to our Lord. Do not grieve, for the joy of the LORD is your strength'" (Nehemiah 8:10).
	"'Until now you have not asked for anything in my name. Ask and you will receive, and your joy will be complete'" (John 16:24).
Guilt	"In him and through faith in him we may approach God with freedom and confidence" (Ephesians 3:12).
	"If you, O LORD, kept a record of sins, O Lord, who could stand? But with you there is forgiveness; therefore you are feared" (Psalm 130:3,4).

If your family is experiencing a difficult time right now, read Exodus 17:8-13.

This story is a perfect word picture of how we can help one another in times of need. The Israelites were winning as long as Moses held his hands up. When he was tired and drained, he dropped his arms, and the Amalekites would begin to win the battle. Finally he wisely asked for help. Aaron and Hur helped support his arms and the Israelites eventually won the battle.

© 1997 by Gospel Light. Permission to photocopy granted. *The Word on Family*

SESSION TWELVE

FAMILY CRISES

How does this exciting story relate to a family experiencing a crisis?

....
....
....

When you are in battle, in what specific ways can your family support and uphold you?

....
....
....

Think about the times when things have been difficult in your life. Did you ask for and receive help from your family? Why, or why not?

....
....
....

What can you, as a family, do to receive all the help you need to get through a battle?

....
....
....

Spend time in prayer for one another asking for God's strength and comfort in the battles you or the whole family are facing right now. Thank Him for His promises of help, comfort and guidance.

Session 12: "Family Crises"
Date ....

161 © 1997 by Gospel Light. Permission to photocopy granted. *The Word on Family*

Give Junior Highers Meat to Chew!
Junior High Builders

Each reproducible manual has 13 Bible studies with tons of games, activities and clip art for your handouts.

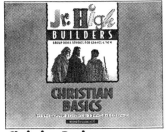
Christian Basics
ISBN 08307.16963

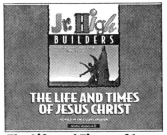
The Life and Times of Jesus Christ
ISBN 08307.16971

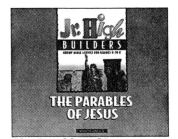
The Parables of Jesus
ISBN 08307.16998

Growing as a Christian
ISBN 08307.17005

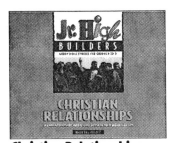
Christian Relationships
ISBN 08307.17013

Symbols of Christ
ISBN 08307.17021

The Power of God
ISBN 08307.17048

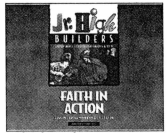
Faith in Action
ISBN 08307.17056

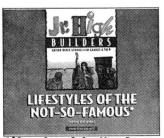
Lifestyles of the Not-So-Famous from the Bible
ISBN 08307.17099

Great Old Testament Leaders
ISBN 08307.17072

Great Truths from Ephesians
ISBN 08307.17080

Peace, Love and Truth
ISBN 08307.17064

Ask for these resources at your local Christian bookstore.

Gospel Light

Take High Schoolers Deep Into God's Word

YouthBuilders Group Bible Studies

These high-involvement, discussion-oriented, Bible-centered studies work together to give you a comprehensive program, seeing your young people through their high school years—and beyond. From respected youth worker Jim Burns.

Give Your Youth *The Word On:*

The Basics of Christianity
ISBN 08307.16440

Being a Leader, Serving Others & Sharing Your Faith
ISBN 08307.16459

Finding and Using Your Spiritual Gifts
ISBN 08307.17897

Helping Friends in Crisis
ISBN 08307.16467

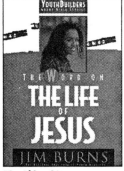

The Life of Jesus
ISBN 08307.16475

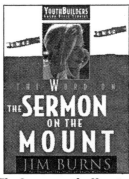

The Sermon on the Mount
ISBN 08307.17234

Prayer and the Devotional Life
ISBN 08307.16432

Sex, Drugs & Rock 'N' Roll
ISBN 08307.16424

Spiritual Warfare
ISBN 08307.17242

The New Testament
ISBN 08307.17250

The Old Testament
ISBN 08307.17269

Family
ISBN 08307.17277

Ask for these resources at your local Christian bookstore.

Gospel Light

Youth Ministry Resources from Gospel Light

YouthBuilders Group Bible Studies

The Word on:

Sex, Drugs and Rock 'N' Roll
ISBN 08307.16424

Prayer and the Devotional Life
ISBN 08307.16432

Basics of Christianity
ISBN 08307.16440

Being a Leader, Serving Others & Sharing Your Faith
ISBN 08307.16459

Helping Friends in Crisis
ISBN 08307.16467

The Life of Jesus
ISBN 08307.16475

Finding and Using Your Spiritual Gifts
ISBN 08307.17897

The Sermon on the Mount
ISBN 08307.17234

Spiritual Warfare
ISBN 08307.17242

The New Testament
ISBN 08307.17250

The Old Testament
ISBN 08307.17269

Family

Jr. High Builders

Christian Basics
ISBN 08307.16963

The Life and Times of Jesus Christ
ISBN 08307.16971

The Parables of Jesus
ISBN 08307.16998

Growing as a Christian
ISBN 08307.17005

Christian Relationships
ISBN 08307.17013

Symbols of Christ
ISBN 08307.17021

The Power of God
ISBN 08307.17048

Faith in Action
ISBN 08307.17056

Peace, Love and Truth
ISBN 08307.17064

Great Old Testament Leaders
ISBN 08307.17072

Great Truths from Ephesians
ISBN 08307.17080

Lifestyles of the Not-So-Famous from the Bible
ISBN 08307.17099

Generation Next
George Barna

Find out how to reach today's teens during this critical period in their lives. Help them cut through confusion and find honest answers to the questions they have.

Hardcover • ISBN 08307.17870

My Family, My Friends, My Life

This powerful 12-session study helps youth understand God's plan for relationships, starting with their own families. Includes reproducible student pages and "Parent Page" to take lessons into the home.

Manual • ISBN 08307.16947

Micro Messages
Tom Finley and Rick Bundschuh

30 quick, complete one-page messages, each featuring accompanying evangelism tracts with an attitude.

Manual • ISBN 08307.15789

The Youthworker's Book of Case Studies
Jim Burns

Fifty-two true stories with discussion questions to add interest to any Bible study.

Manual • ISBN 08307.15827

Show Youth Their Identity in Christ

Stomping Out the Darkness
Neil T. Anderson and Dave Park

Here is the powerful message from **Victory over the Darkness** written especially for young people that provides youth with keys to their identity, worth, and acceptance as children of God.

Paperback • ISBN 08307.16408
Study Guide • ISBN 08307.17455

Busting Free
Neil T. Anderson and Dave Park

This youth group study helps young people find biblical solutions to the personal and spiritual wounds that cripple their self-esteem and confuse their identity.

Manual • ISBN 08307.16653
Video Seminar • UPC 607135.000808

Outrageous Object Lessons
E. G. VonTrutzschler

Do you teach using mousetraps, birds and seeds? Jesus and Jeremiah often used object lessons and you can too! Teaching tools—from the simple to the outrageous—present Bible principles in vibrant, new ways.

Manual • ISBN 08307.14960

Super Clip Art for Youth Workers on Disk
Tom Finley

The latest high-quality clip art to supercharge flyers and newsletters. Includes disks, instructions and book.

Windows Disks • SPCN 25116.06607
Macintosh Disks • SPCN 25116.06593
Win/Mac CD-ROM • UPC 607135.002604

Ask for these resources at your local Christian bookstore

Gospel Light

HIGH POWERED YOUTH SEMINARS WITH JIM BURNS

Challenge your group to make their lives count for Christ as you help lay a firm foundation for their future. Here are resources to help your kids make a difference in the world.

Radical Christianity
Book & Video
Jim Burns

Radical Christianity is a proven plan to help young people live a life that's worth living and make a difference in their world.
ISBN 08307.17927 • $9.99
Paperback

SPCN 85116.01082
$19.99 • VHS Video

Radical Love
Book & Video
Jim Burns

In Radical Love kids discover why it's best to wait on God's timing, how to say "no" when their body says "yes" and how to find forgiveness for past mistakes.
ISBN 08307.17935 • $9.99
Paperback

SPCN 85116.00922
$19.99 • VHS Video

Each Book has questions and exercises for each chapter that are great for any size group study.

Each 90 minute video has 3 -half hour messages presented by Jim Burns each with a reproducible lesson plan and viewing outline.

More resources for youth leaders:

Steering Them Straight
Stephen Arterburn & Jim Burns
Parents can find understanding as well as practical tools to deal with crisis situations. Includes guidelines that will help any family prevent problems before they develop.
ISBN 1-5617-940-66
$10.95

The Youth Builder
Jim Burns
This Gold Medallion Award winner provides you with proven methods, specific recommendations and hands-on examples of handling and understanding the problems and challenges of youth ministry.
ISBN 0-89081-576-3
$16.95

Getting in Touch with God
Jim Burns
Develop a consistent and disciplined time with God in the midst of hectic schedules as Jim Burns shares with you inspiring devotional readings to deepen your love for God.
ISBN 0-89081-520-8
$5.95

Dear Dad, If I Could Tell You Anything
Doug Webster
For every father who wants to better understand his child. These touching and inspirational messages will enable you to draw closer to your child by discovering what he or she thinks, feels and needs.
ISBN 0-78528-079-0
$12.95

High School Ministry
Mike Yaconelli & Jim Burns
Especially written for high-school youth workers—learn about the youth and the influence of their culture and discover the tremendous impact you can have on your kids.
ISBN 0-31031-921-1
$12.95

Spirit Wings
Jim Burns
In the language of today's teens, these 84 short devotionals will encourage youth to build a stronger and more intimate relationship with God.
ISBN 0-89283-783-7
$10.95

Dear Mom If I Could Tell You Anything
Robin Webster and Doug Webster
By exposing the question, "If you could tell your mom anything, what would you say," gives moms the opportunity hear what kids are really thinking and feeling and presents ways for parents to understand and meet the needs of their kids.
ISBN 0-78527-589-4
$14.95

To order NIYM resources, please call
1-800-397-9725
or to learn how you can take advantage of NIYM training opportunities call or write to:
NIYM • POBox 4374 • San Clemente CA 92674 • 714/498-4418

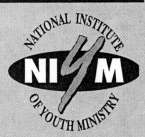

Youth Worker IQ Test:

What in the world is *NIYM*?

- A.) The Neurotically Inclined Yo-Yo Masters
- B.) The Neatest Incidental Yearbook Mystery
- C.) The Natural Ignition Yields of Marshmallows
- D.) The National Institute of Youth Ministry

If you deliberately picked *A*, *B*, or *C* you're the reason Jim Burns started NIYM! If you picked *D*, you can go to the next page. In any case, you could learn more about NIYM. Here are some IQ score-raisers:

Jim Burns started NIYM to:
- Meet the growing needs of training and equipping youth workers and parents
- Develop excellent resources and events for young people—in the U.S. and internationally
- Empower young people and their families to make wise decisions and experience a vital Christian lifestyle.

NIYM can make a difference in your life and enhance your youth work skills through these special events:

Institutes—These consist of week-long, in-depth small-group training sessions for youth workers.

Trainer of Trainees—NIYM will train you to train others. You can use this training with your volunteers, parents and denominational events. You can go through the certification process and become an official NIYM associate. (No, you don't get a badge or decoder ring).

International Training—Join NIYM associates to bring youth ministry to kids and adults around the world. (You'll learn meanings to universal words like "yo!" and "hey!")

Custom Training—These are special training events for denominational groups, churches, networks, colleges and seminaries.

Parent Forums—We'll come to your church or community with two incredible hours of learning, interaction and fellowship. It'll be fun finding out who makes your kids tick!

Youth Events—Dynamic speakers, interaction and drama bring a powerful message to kids through a fun and fast-paced day. Our youth events include: This Side Up, Radical Respect, Surviving Adolescence and Peer Leadership.

For brain food or a free information packet about the National Institute of Youth Ministry, write to:

NIYM
P.O. Box 4374 • San Clemente, CA 92674
Tel: (714) 498-4418 • Fax: (714) 498-0037 • NIYMin@aol.com